Restricting Los Angeles Paparazzi

Restricting Los Angeles Paparazzi

California's Legal Efforts Impacting Free Press Rights

Joshua N. Azriel

LEXINGTON BOOKS
Lanham • Boulder • New York • London

Published by Lexington Books
An imprint of The Rowman & Littlefield Publishing Group, Inc.
4501 Forbes Boulevard, Suite 200, Lanham, Maryland 20706
www.rowman.com

6 Tinworth Street, London SE11 5AL, United Kingdom

British Library Cataloguing in Publication Information Available

Library of Congress Cataloging-in-Publication Data Available
Library of Congress Control Number: 2020944711

ISBN 978-1-4985-7897-4 (cloth)
ISBN 978-1-4985-7898-1 (electronic)

Contents

Acknowledgments

In 2014, I read a newspaper article about California's Governor Jerry Brown signing legislation called the "anti-paparazzi" law. The article discussed how celebrities were fighting back against paparazzi intrusion into their families' lives. They were angry about their under-age children's images being photographed and published. That article led me to a basic question: What did the law actually say about protecting the public's privacy? After reading it, several First Amendment, freedom of press challenges to the law become apparent. Reading the state's anti-paparazzi laws put me on a research journey that included publishing academic articles that, in turn, led to the genesis of this book project

This book is based on a personal fascination with Hollywood celebrity culture and the role of the paparazzi within it. How we define celebrities keeps changing, especially in the world of reality television. As someone who lives outside California, it was important for me to interview experts who worked in the entertainment journalism profession in order to get a firsthand understanding of the relationships between celebrities and paparazzi. I quickly realized there would be a field research component to this project. Spending six days in Los Angeles, California, working as a paparazzo and interviewing photographers provided an up-close-and-personal view of the celebrity-photographer relationship. I promised confidentiality to those who introduced me to the paparazzi profession, and I am grateful to them. The field research conducted for this book will provide students with firsthand expertise by those who work as paparazzi.

Earning a living as a paparazzo is hard. The work is mostly outside, on your feet at least ten hours per day regardless of weather conditions. There is no stable income and photographers do not know on any day how much money they will earn from their photos. An important part of the business is simply getting lucky with one photo that can pay thousands of dollars. Essentially, it is about being at the right place at the right time. The field research for this book simply would not have been possible without those photographers who walk the streets of Los Angeles and assisted me with important advice on whom to interview.

This project has been a labor of love. It exposed me to a professional culture different from my current academic one and quite different from my previous work as a journalist. While not all paparazzi were friendly or willing to talk, most treated me with respect and gave me a peek into their professional culture. As an academic, I am lucky to be able to work on different research projects that introduce me to the larger media world.

This book would not have been possible without the advice of two key colleagues. Kennesaw State University professors Dr. Amber Hutchins and Dr. Jefferson DeWitt provided lots of great ideas. Dr. Hutchins challenged me to think about what celebrity fundamentally means and was a wonderful source of research materials. Dr. DeWitt assisted with giving me ideas for interview questions that focused on how California's anti-paparazzi laws impact paparazzi. We thought about questions from both quantitative and qualitative perspectives.

Dr. Carolyn Carlson did an outstanding job in editing my book, and she challenged me to think critically about my definition of celebrity. I also want to acknowledge the support of Kennesaw State University's School of Communication and Media Director Dr. Barbara Gainey. She assisted with providing teaching flexibility in order to have time to write. A special thank-you to Tenisha Bell, without whom I would have struggled with some initial Los Angeles media contacts. My graduate assistant Odera Ezenna assisted with setting up my iPad with software to conduct the interviews and assisted me with writing many of the interview questions. I am honored that Dr. Charles Davis, the Dean of the Grady College of Journalism and Mass Communication at the University of Georgia, wrote the foreword for this book.

On a personal note, I need to thank my wife, journalist Michelle Azriel. I asked her to read my first completed draft. She was vital in assisting me in editing my copy into a more active voice. We sat together at our kitchen table reading through each chapter debating the meaning of words. Her sage advice helped me sharpen the meaning of several parts of this book.

The editors at Lexington Books were great to work with. Nicolette Amstutz and Jessica Tepper, the acquisitions editors, kept reminding me to engage with the existing scholarship in the area of paparazzi research while embracing the qualitative methodology used for the field research. It is my hope that this book will be read by journalism and media students. It can serve as a case study in freedom of the press, journalism ethics, and privacy issues. Paparazzi in Los Angeles play a direct role in our celebrity culture. They provide content for our "appetite" to see and learn more about our favorite stars. Yet, there are causes for serious concern from First Amendment freedom of speech and press perspectives. Paparazzi are media and more specifically, journalists. Any law aimed at their profession needs to be treated with a certain amount of skepticism unless it is narrowly written in a way that it does not interfere with their basic rights as photographers. I hope students can apply what they read in this book to the larger professional world in which they aspire to one day work.

Foreword

One typically picturesque day in Beverly Hills, I was frightened by a small horde of paparazzi who descended on a gentleman walking ahead of me. An infrequent visitor to Los Angeles, I had longed for a celebrity-spotting moment—and here it was, yet I couldn't enjoy it because I didn't quite know what was happening and I had no earthly idea who the person in front of me was.

I asked one of the photographers, who condescendingly sneered, "My God, man, its Mark Wahlberg."

And with that, I had my lone interaction with paparazzi in the wild.

I had momentarily been a bystander to a time-honored Hollywood ritual, one decried—and cleverly deployed—by celebrities since the dawn of photography. The stalking, the flash popping, the sulking star(let), all so formulaic, like watching a real-life version of a timeworn television show.

The mere mention of the term *paparazzi* engenders such disgust among many that scholarly analysis of the phenomenon remains scarce. Paparazzi occupy a page or so of every media law text in existence, delineating the parameters of legitimate newsgathering and illegitimate intrusion before inevitably turning to the paparazzi incident that short-circuits any nuanced analysis of the issue, Princess Diana.

That harrowing 1997 incident, in which a speeding car carrying Diana away from the paparazzi crashed into a pillar, killing her and her then-fiancé Dodi al-Fayed, enraged millions who lay blame for the beloved royal's death squarely on the photographers.

At her funeral in September 1997, her brother Charles Spencer left mourners in no doubt whom he blamed, describing his sister as "the most hunted person of the modern age." "She would want us today to pledge ourselves to protecting her beloved boys, William and Harry, from a similar fate," he said. "We will not allow them to suffer the anguish that used regularly to drive you to tearful despair."

The public mood turned radically against the paparazzi, and the UK enacted laws making their lives immeasurably harder. In the United States, though, similar efforts raise very real First Amendment issues. While popular opinion of paparazzi remains low, the public's seemingly insatiable appetite for celebrity pics continues to fuel the cat-and-mouse game. The relationship between paparazzi and their subjects, never warm and fuzzy, often turns confrontational, and the meteoric rise of social media, clickbait celebrity websites and other players have blurred the lines even further.

Celebrity spotting these days certainly includes paparazzi, but also anyone nearby with a cell phone. And celebrities now can control more of their own imagery through the clever use of Instagram to build their following and offer their own photography as competition to the paparazzi.

Against this rapidly changing backdrop, Joshua Azriel's work attempts to place the paparazzi in its proper First Amendment context, and by doing so, to help us better understand this murky area of celebrity journalism. Through extensive interviews with paparazzi, editors and field producers, First Amendment attorneys and reporters, Azriel takes the reader behind the scenes, all the while carefully laying out the historical and legal foundations of the industry.

Through the use of a novel and wildly entertaining week in the shoes of a paparazzo, Azriel's first-person ethnography takes the reader to the streets of Hollywood, bringing doctrinal legal research to life. The result is a lively examination of what it's like to work as a paparazzo, a chapter sure to humanize these oft-reviled photographers making a living supplying the world's booming market for celebrity news and imagery.

Like it or not, paparazzi engage in a whole host of protected forms of newsgathering, and perform in many ways like the rest of the press. Their more infamous outliers challenge notions of personal privacy, to be sure. But this book is a reminder of the complexity inherent in many newsgathering situations, where public figures in public places seek the protection of privacy laws, mostly unsuccessfully. For ours is a nation protective of the principle that we'd rather not succumb to the impulse to censor, that what happens in public is, after all, public. Warts and all, paparazzi play a role in a free-wheeling national discourse, one that the United Supreme Court famously said should be "uninhibited, robust and wide-open."

This book is timely reminder of that age-old proclamation, and a scholarly treatise on a too-often-overlooked area of media law. It's a history, legal and societal, a discourse on changing mores and on the impact of one small piece of the larger media ecosystem on the whole of press freedom. That is its lasting message to this reader: that a free press is free only when its ragged edges are protected from the impulse to censor.

—Dr. Charles Davis
Dean, Grady School of Journalism and Mass Communication
University of Georgia

Introduction

Paparazzi. You either love them or hate them. For the consumer, paparazzi are the literal and figurative lens through which we see our favorite celebrities in "real life" while we briefly disconnect from our real lives and seek out distractions. Information about celebrities is often that distraction. For celebrities, paparazzi can be intrusive but at the same time, they need these photographers to keep their career in the public eye. For the paparazzi themselves, they often feel misunderstood. They are at the center of how celebrities promote themselves for the public's "guilty pleasure" of viewing their lives.

The celebrity relationship with the paparazzi world is complicated. There are famous parents who understandably want a zone of privacy for their children. Others, including many reality stars, often embrace the exposure while many celebrities just go about their lives ignoring the cameras. These are just a few quotes given by celebrities about their interactions with paparazzi.

> I knew the paparazzi were going to be a reality in my life, but I didn't know that I would feel anxiety every time I open my front door, or that being chased by 10 men you don't know, or being surrounded, feels invasive and makes me feel scared and gets my adrenaline going every day. —Jennifer Lawrence (2017)[1]

> I really feel like I play so fair with the media all the time and I'm super gracious with everybody and all I ask is them to stay away from my kids and that one little—like when I got home, just let me go home. It's disrespectful. I don't want people around my kids like that, in that way. —Jennifer Lopez (2017)[2]

> You're a piece of trash. Stay away from my wife. Shut up! You're a piece of garbage! —Alec Baldwin (2016)[3]

> Picture what it would be like walking down the street with your child, whether it's trick or treating or just to school, and have ten aggressive men taking their picture with a lens in your face, yelling, pushing other children outside of a school. —Kristen Bell (2014)[4]

> I got surrounded by these photographers and they were flashing. . . . I started crying and saying "Stop! Stop! Stop!" —Minnie Driver (2014)[5]

Those stars' frustrations are echoed by many celebrities. Complaints about a lack of personal and family privacy are heard in the main paparazzi locations around the world: London, New York, and Los Angeles.

Paparazzi roaming specific areas of these cities where celebrities are known to live and work is part of the culture of the entertainment business.

Celebrities who believe their lives are saturated by paparazzi stalking them have fought back using mass media. Lady Gaga, Britney Spears, and Michael Jackson wrote songs and produced videos to convey their frustrations. Others, such as Alec Baldwin and Brad Pitt, had open confrontations with the photographers; whereas Kristen Bell and her husband, Dax Shepard led a successful Twitter campaign in 2014 to force media companies to respect the privacy of celebrity children. In 2013 Halle Berry and Jennifer Garner testified before the California State Assembly in a successful effort to have a state law passed to protect their families' privacy.

The music lyrics written by Lady Gaga and Britney Spears pointedly reflected their frustrations with the paparazzi constantly trailing them. In Spears's song, "Piece of Me," her lyrics are a sharp criticism of the paparazzi industry with words such as: "They still gon' put pictures of my derriere in the magazine" and "You want a piece of me."[6] The accompanying music video to "Piece of Me" has images of flashing camera bulbs from paparazzi photographing her and literally chasing after her to capture a photo. The song and video were produced after Spears's infamous incident of the paparazzi taking her photograph while she shaved her head.

Lady Gaga's video based on the song "Paparazzi" satirized the paparazzi. Her song lyrics were from the perspective of the photographers, who say to her character, "I'm your biggest fan" and "I'll follow you until you love me."[7] In the accompanying video, Lady Gaga's character is an exaggerated version of herself as a celebrity musician who reached the pinnacle of her career. The paparazzi take photos of her outside her mansion. They follow her character's professional ups and downs, always demanding photos. Similar to Spears's video, it has the ongoing flash of the camera as Lady Gaga's career is tracked by the paparazzi.

While musicians can use their medium to critique the paparazzi, some celebrities actually seek out the paparazzi. Publicists will discreetly contact photographers and tell them where their celebrity client will be at a given time. This sought-after publicity is often connected to the release of an upcoming project. Other times, stars or their publicists use the paparazzi to attempt to control the personal image or narrative they want to convey. This is often carefully choreographed. Fundamentally, the relationship between the paparazzi and celebrities is no mystery. Many photographers say the two groups need each other. Celebrities need the publicity, and the photographers are happy to provide it. Their compensation is indirectly based on the public's demand for those photos.

Paparazzi, as a term, originated in Italy. Movie director Federico Fellini invented the word while directing the film *La Dolce Vita*. In the movie, the paparazzi were the photographers who hounded famous people. The word *paparazzi* translates to annoying mosquitoes.[8] *La Dolce Vita* reflected the status of celebrity photographers in Italy. The movie's main character, Paparazzo, follows stars around Rome "annoying them like pests."[9] In reality, 1950s celebrity photographers chased after actors who were filming movies in and around Rome. They were famous for riding scooters (often in packs) around the city looking for celebrities to photograph.

The stories from the 1950s of paparazzi chasing after actors Richard Burton and Elizabeth Taylor are what we often associate paparazzi with today. We have all seen the images of a head-shaven Britney Spears taunting photographers who surrounded her car in 2007. No one can forget the chase that culminated in Princess Diana's death in 1997. It is no surprise when Alec Baldwin has a run-in with photographers in New York City. While these infamous incidents reflect a paparazzi culture often out of control, most photographers quietly go about their business tracking down celebrities. Just as many journalists work a beat and have sources who relay information, paparazzi have favorite locations and trusted informants and quietly do their job.

Paparazzi photography is not traditional photojournalism. It exists to photograph celebrities and to sell the photos. Stylistically, it is a combination of four types of photography: surveillance, celebrity, documentary, and journalism.[10] The purpose of this unique form of photography is to give the consumer brief access to a celebrity's life.[11] A vast majority of the photographs we see of celebrities is a slice of their daily lives: running errands and spending time with family. Beyond the formal events and parties, we like to see them live a "normal life."

Celebrity photography is a business. It functions on the simple notion of supply and demand. When demand for celebrity photos is high and supply is low, then more money is paid to the paparazzo for the photograph. When demand is low and supply is high, the value for the photographs declines. Essentially, celebrities are public figures who have a value to their image. That value fluctuates. There are some celebrities whose values remain high, such as Brad Pitt, Angelina Jolie, and Julia Roberts. Often, an unforeseen death causes the value of an image to rise dramatically. For example, Christopher Weiss, the paparazzo who captured an image of Michael Jackson's dead body, earned hundreds of thousands of dollars for that last photo.[12] Paparazzi who earned thousands of dollars *per day* a decade ago now earn about the same amount of money *per week*. It is often said paparazzi "work twice as hard for half of the money" compared to ten years ago.[13] They now earn about 80 percent less from their photographs.[14] Others have left the celebrity photography business and have put their visual skills to other, more mainstream uses.

In recent years, celebrities' own Instagram accounts have become direct competition for the paparazzi. Television, magazines, and online celebrity sites are co-opting photos from celebrities' public Instagram sites and are no longer relying on paparazzi-generated photographs. For example, Wendy Williams, the host of the *Wendy Williams Show*, uses celebrities' own Instagram photos as part of her "Hot Topics" segment.[15] Ironically, as a celebrity show host, she is also the frequent target of the paparazzi cameras.[16] Williams's show, similar to many other entertainment-focused programs, utilizes both paparazzi and Instagram accounts for her celebrity-focused segment. Another example is ABC's *Good Morning America*. It often uses celebrity-sourced images for its entertainment stories.

Paparazzi admit that social media, Instagram specifically, is now their direct competition. They no longer receive high earnings from their photos when the same celebrity photo subjects are providing their own.[17] Celebrities often provide their own exclusives and essentially beat out the paparazzi. Easy access to social media from our cell phones makes it easy for any celebrity to be his or her own publicist and more importantly, avoid needing the paparazzi for those photos they want their fans to see. Ironically, the result is that the supply of photos from the celebrities themselves compete with those provided by paparazzi. This leads to a decrease in paparazzi earnings. Photographers are no longer the exclusive source of the "real-life" photos celebrities portray to the public. What was once the paparazzi's exclusive domain is now shared with the celebrity subjects they also follow. In essence, paparazzi are often in direct competition with the same celebrities they photograph.

The financial pressures on paparazzi in Los Angeles is compounded by laws that in recent years have targeted the industry. In 2013, Halle Berry and Jennifer Garner testified before the California Assembly that paparazzi intrusion into their children's lives was out of control. They stated that their children were photographed without permission, and their children had become scared of the paparazzi.[18] In 2014 former Governor Jerry Brown signed into law two major updates to the state's privacy and anti-harassment laws.[19] Each law imposed fines on paparazzi who are accused and found guilty of violating someone's family privacy or harassing and stalking them. Taken together, these are often referred to as the anti-paparazzi laws.

At the same time in 2014 actress Kristen Bell led a public Twitter campaign warning television shows and magazines that she and her husband, Dax Shepard would not allow themselves to be interviewed unless there was a promise made to exclude their children from photographs and videos.[20] Many other celebrities, including Eric Dane and Minnie Driver, joined this effort.[21] Bell successfully leveraged the power of social media communication to pressure entertainment media to respect the stars' wishes. These media companies knew that the more celebrities who came forward and supported Bell and her husband, the less access they would have to the very people they needed for producing content for the public. In turn, that would affect their profit margins. Bell considered her effort a personal success with far fewer paparazzi taking photos of actors' children in recent years. Bell stated, "I've heard from entertainers with a bigger profile that it made a difference in their lives and that their children are less paranoid because they're not being hunted by a strange group of men and women."[22]

The combination of both the 2014 anti-paparazzi law and Bell's Twitter campaign impacted how paparazzi now do their jobs in Los Angeles. In a series of interviews for this book, paparazzi indicated that many try not to cross a legal line and invade the privacy of celebrities and their families.[23] One photographer simply said, "It's a job."[24] It is the means by which he earns money with his camera. Yet, that paparazzo said he feels the constant pressure not to cross a line of snapping photos of celebrities' families. There are still photographers who will try and take photos of children, but they are far fewer in number now than years ago.

California's attempts to regulate paparazzi behavior is controversial. From one perspective, the public, including celebrities, deserve to live their lives privately at home *and* when they are out in public *with* their children. Yet, at the same time, celebrities have fewer privacy rights when they are seen in public. As actors, directors, athletes, and reality television stars, they often do their jobs in the public eye. The job of a paparazzo is to take photos and videos. Paparazzi say they satisfy the public's demand for these images. They argue that the public's desire for these photos fuels the market demand. They simply provide the content for that demand. On top of this dynamic are laws that are well-meaning but at the same time must safeguard the photographers' First Amendment freedom of press rights.

Both Sections 1708.7 and 1708.8 of the California Civil Code are complex laws that will be analyzed in this book. Their purpose is to ensure that the paparazzi do not step over a red line in their quest to take celebrity images even though the law applies to every state resident. This book will explore the controversial parts of the laws that directly impact the media, specifically paparazzi. Love them or hate them, freedom of the press is a legal safeguard for them. The main question is whether the California laws violate paparazzi freedom of the press in marked contrast to a long legal tradition of a free press in the United States. This book is a case study that will demonstrate that paparazzi are press and fully protected under the First Amendment.

As this book will explain, there are very few legal restrictions placed on the press in the United States. Censorship rarely happens, and when it does it is always on the burden of the government to justify it. We have a presumption that censorship or prior restraint upon the press is illegal. The rare cases of justified censorship occur when national security is threatened or there is a danger to a defendant's right to a fair trial.[25] In the world of celebrity journalism, calls for censorship occur within the realm of protecting a celebrity's physical privacy. Celebrities often call for censorship when their physical space is invaded, and threaten legal action if, for example, their private health information is publicized. Those calls for censorship usually occur *after* a private image or piece of information is published. Once that private and possibly embarrassing information is made public, there is no way to erase that information from the marketplace of ideas. The celebrity must then convey a narrative that competes with the false or private information.

Dozens of photographers staking out someone's home and impeding the celebrity's ability to leave may be met with a legal threat of action. Yet, generally, the government at the federal or state level cannot censor the media. This includes California, the state home to a vast multibillion-dollar entertainment industry and to the stars who live and work there. Los Angeles and its surrounding communities are the epicenter of the state's paparazzi presence. The photos we often see of a celebrity walking down the street with a Starbucks in hand or entering and exiting the gym after a workout are usually from in and around Los Angeles, not from other cities in California.

This book explores Los Angeles, California–based paparazzi from First Amendment freedom of speech and freedom of press contexts. It will examine paparazzi rights from different perspectives: journalists, media industry insiders, and most importantly, the paparazzi themselves. This author was given access to professionals in this industry. Extensive interviews were held with both current and retired paparazzi photographers, editors, and field producers. Reporters who work in the entertainment industry were interviewed, as well as attorneys whose work focuses on First Amendment free press issues including California's anti-paparazzi laws. The data gathered for this book was conducted in Los Angeles while working as a freelance paparazzo for one week. The author engaged in ethnographic participant-observation for this book. Paparazzi were observed, photographed, and interviewed on their celebrity beats.

Chapter 1 is an overview of the professional world of the paparazzi and their interactions with celebrities. Chapter 2 provides viewpoints about the paparazzi from mainstream entertainment journalists. Chapter 3 analyzes California's three anti-paparazzi laws that focus on invasion of privacy, stalking, and reckless driving. Chapter 4 provides the results of field interviews conducted with paparazzi as they staked out celebrities in the field. Chapter 5 is a more personal perspective of the author's experience as a pseudo-paparazzo photographer for one week in Los Angeles. Finally, chapter 6 concludes with legal recommendations about how to balance the First Amendment rights of paparazzi, the media they serve, and the rights of celebrities and their families. It offers solutions to guarantee paparazzi press rights within the context of protecting individuals' privacy and reducing the risk of harm from harassment. The suggestions for how the California Assembly can amend the laws are aimed at avoiding the inevitable, future legal challenges in state or federal courts. It is likely that at some point in the future, a media organization or individual paparazzo will sue to have parts of the laws overturned because they violate the First Amendment's freedom of press rights.

NOTES

1. Bridget Burns, "13 Celebrities on Protecting Their Privacy," *Marie Claire*, August 2, 2017, https://www.marieclaire.com/celebrity/news/g4914/celebrities-privacy-quotes/.
2. Alexa, Tietjin, "Jennifer Lopez Blasts Paparazzi After Photo Goes Viral," *WWD*, March 2, 2017, https://wwd.com/eye/parties/jennifer-lopez-blasts-paparazzi-photo-viral-10828622/.
3. Jasmine Stone, "Everyone Loves It When Alec Baldwin Has a Paparazzi Meltdown," *2 Oceans Vibe News*, May 6, 2016, https://www.2oceansvibe.com/2016/05/06/everyone-loves-it-when-alec-baldwin-has-a-paparazzi-meltdown-video/.
4. "Kristen Bell and Dax Shepherd lead campaign to protect kids from paparazzi," *CBSnews.com*, February 28, 2014, https://www.cbsnews.com/news/kristen-bell-and-dax-shepard-start-campagin-to-protect-children-from-paparazzi/.
5. "More Stars Join 'No Kids Policy' Paparazzi Fight," *ETonline*, February 26, 2014, https://www.etonline.com/news/143823_More_Stars_Join_No_Kids_Policy_Paparazzi_Fight.
6. Spears, Britney. *Piece of Me*. Jive Records. Originally released November 27, 2007.
7. Lady Gaga, *Paparazzi*. Interscope Records. Originally released July 6, 2009.
8. Clément Chéroux, "Thirteen and a Half Theories on the Concept of Paparazzi Photography," *Paparazzi! Photographers, Stars, Artists* ed. Clément Chéroux, (France: Flammarion, 2014), 13.
9. Kim McNamara, *Paparazzi: Media Practices and Celebrity Culture* (Malden, MA: Polity 2016), 13.
10. Carol Squiers, "Class Struggle: The Invention of Paparazzi Photography and the Death of Dina, Princess of Wales," *Overexposed: Essays on Contemporary Photography*, ed. Carol Squiers, (New York: The New Press, 1999), 271.
11. Ibid.
12. Michael Joseph Gross, "Michael Jackson's Last Close-Up," *Vanity Fair* June 1, 2009.
13. Many of the paparazzi interviewed for this book complained about their shrinking incomes from celebrity photographs.
14. The estimate of an 80 percent reduction in compensation is based on two in-depth interviews with Giles Harrison and Vince Flores.
15. David Marchese, "Wendy Williams Wants to Be the Realest in the Game," *The New York Times Magazine*, August 26, 2019, https://www.nytimes.com/interactive/2019/08/26/magazine/wendy-williams-interview.html?smid=nytcore-ios-share.
16. Ibid.
17. Interviews with twelve paparazzi photographers, July 2019.
18. "Halle Berry happy about anti-paparazzi bill passage," *USA Today*, September 25, 2013, https://www.usatoday.com/story/life/people/2013/09/25/california-gov-jerry-brown-signs-anti-paparazzi-bill/2870965/.
19. Cal. Civ. Code §1708.8 (2018) and Cal. Civ. Code §1708.7 (2018).
20. Kristen Bell uses the Twitter handle @IMKristenBell, and Dax Shepard's Twitter handle is @daxshepherd1. In 2014 they launched a series of Twitter hashtags including #FirstAmendment, #PhotographersGoneWild, and #pedorazzi in their desire to limit paparazzi intrusion into celebrities' children's lives.

21. "More Stars Join 'No Kids Policy' Paparazzi Fight," *ETonline*, February 26, 2014, https://www.etonline.com/news/143823_More_Stars_Join_No_Kids_Policy_Paparazzi_Fight.

22. Carly Milne, "Kristen Bell on the Paparazzi Stalking Children: 'I Saw a Problem, Attacked It Like a Mother, and Actually Made a Difference,'" *Yahoo! Entertainment*, May 6, 2016, https://www.yahoo.com/entertainment/kristen-bell-on-the-paparazzi-stalking-children-005049108.html.

23. Interviews with twelve paparazzi photographers, July 2019.

24. Interview with an anonymous paparazzo in Studio City, CA (July 14, 2019).

25. U.S. Const. amend. VI.

ONE

The Paparazzi and Celebrity Worlds

Imagine the peace of a quiet neighborhood that's shattered after a television star or athlete moves in next door or across the street. You wake up the next day to find the street in front of your new neighbor's home now crowded with photographers and their cars. Leaving your own driveway is no longer simple. Actress Jennifer Aniston complained about this very issue with paparazzi stalking her Los Angeles area home every day, causing traffic problems for the neighborhood.[1]

Jennifer Garner testified before the California State Assembly that cars surround her home on a daily basis, and paparazzi often track her daily family activities with her children. She described paparazzi activities as a "mob scene."[2] Garner contended this was a constant occurrence for her family. She has explained to her young children why men they do not know follow them with cameras.[3]

What if you are a celebrity promoting an upcoming movie, and paparazzi literally swarm you and prevent you from walking? This happened to Scarlett Johansson in April 2019 moments after she appeared on *Jimmy Kimmel Live!* promoting *Avengers: Endgame* as she exited the studio.[4] Her security detail drove her to the Los Angeles Police Department's Hollywood station to wait for the photographers to disperse.[5]

What if you are going out to dinner and you see more than a dozen photographers standing outside the restaurant? As you walk toward the entrance, the flashes from the paparazzi's cameras momentarily blind you since a celebrity is leaving the restaurant. This is likely to happen almost any night at Craig's in Beverly Hills.

Now visualize driving on a highway in your hometown and two cars race past you, weaving and bobbing in traffic at speeds of 80 miles per hour and higher. It would be normal to think that both drivers may be on their way to the hospital due to a medical emergency. What if you found out that a pop star was driving the first car with a photographer quickly following behind? The cameraman at the wheel actively took photos as he sped after the singer. Singer Justin Bieber was involved in this very scenario.

In 2012 paparazzo Paul Raef was directly involved in a motor chase with Justin Bieber on a Los Angeles road.[6] Raef was driving his car and taking pictures at the same time. Luckily, a major accident similar to the 1997 paparazzi chase that killed Princess Diana and her boyfriend, Dodi Fayed, did not happen between Raef and Bieber. The public blamed the paparazzi for Diana's death then, and fifteen years later blamed them for putting thousands of Los Angeles motorists in harm's way in the Bieber chase. In these cases, it can be argued that our tabloid culture is to blame. It empowers the paparazzi to take reckless actions.[7] Paparazzi chasing down celebrities is not a recent phenomenon.

In the early 1960s Italian paparazzi were notorious for following Elizabeth Taylor and Richard Burton while they filmed *Cleopatra*.[8] They were both married but hiding their affair. One of the paparazzi incidents led to Burton and Taylor driving a car into a ditch. They blamed the paparazzi for the accident. In the Raef–Bieber driving incident, Raef was arrested and charged with violating a California vehicle law that prohibited reckless driving on streets and highways while photographing a subject.[9]

Italian filmmaker Federico Fellini coined the term *paparazzi* in his film *La Dolce Vita*. The 1960 fictional film mirrored real-life paparazzi activity in Rome. The film's story focused on an actress who was hounded by a photographer character named Paparazzo. In Italian, *paparazzo* translates as "buzzing mosquito." Fast-forward more than fifty years later, whether we consider paparazzi photography as a form of celebrity photojournalism or the likes of annoying, *buzzing mosquitos* is not as important as their legal right to do their jobs, even if they annoy their celebrity subjects.

The paparazzo's goal is simple: sell photos to earn money. Photography scholar Carol Squiers described the job in a simple way: "Paparazzi photography is considered a bastard branch of editorial photography in which pecuniary gain and social outrage outstrip any concern with aesthetics or content."[10] Media researcher Kim McNamara noted that in order to earn money, paparazzi depend on both skill and luck.[11] Often, they happen to be at the *right place* at the *best time* in the *opportune position* to shoot *the* photo that earns them thousands of dollars.

Several journalism associations, including the National Press Photographers Association, the Reporters Committee for Freedom of the Press, and the Society of Professional Journalists, support paparazzi rights to perform their jobs within the framework of the First Amendment. In the case of Paul Raef chasing after Justin Bieber, these organizations supported Raef's argument that the California Vehicle Code criminalizing any active recording of video, sound, or photography while driving a vehicle was an unconstitutional violation of his First Amendment rights.[12] Yet, the presiding judge in the appeals court decision, Norman Epstein, ruled the law was not explicitly aimed at the media: "On its face, section 40008 is not limited to paparazzi chasing celebrities or reporters gathering news. Instead, the statute targets 'any person' who commits an enumerated traffic offense with the intent to capture the image, sound, or physical impression of 'another person' for a commercial purpose."[13]

The Raef–Bieber chase illustrates that paparazzi believe they are equal to and should be treated as mainstream press. Essentially, they gather information about celebrities by recording videos and taking photographs. Their photos and videos are often broadcast on television programs, published in magazines, and posted on websites and social media accounts affiliated with *TMZ*, *E! News*, *People*, and *In Touch*, just to name a few. One of the most well-known paparazzi media companies, TMZ, considers itself a news organization and entitled to press freedom under the First Amendment. Its owner and founder, Harvey Levin, advocates that he manages a news operation and is, therefore, entitled to press freedom under the First Amendment.[14]

Websites such as *TMZ.com* rely on informants around Hollywood to provide information about celebrity whereabouts.[15] Specifically, TMZ often pays informants at Los Angeles–area hotels, the airport, local police departments, and restaurants for tips about celebrity comings and goings.[16] The Paul Raef–Justin Bieber incident and the paparazzi staking out the homes of celebrities such as Jennifer Aniston do not just occur in a vacuum. Paparazzi can earn a lot of money following celebrities and recording videos and taking photographs. One photographer can earn tens of thousands of dollars from just one photo of an in-demand celebrity.[17]

While paparazzi demand the same legal rights afforded to the mainstream press, many celebrities demand the same privacy rights afforded to the average American. Jennifer Garner, Halle Berry, and Jennifer Aniston are three well-known activists who have led the fight against paparazzi intrusion into their families' lives. Garner and Berry testified before the California legislature in 2013 about paparazzi activities aimed at their children.[18] In 2016 Aniston wrote in a *Huffington Post* blog post about her daily encounters with "dozens of aggressive photographers" who staked out her home in the hopes of landing a photograph of her and now-ex-husband, Justin Theroux.[19] Aniston complained that the paparazzi placed both her and her ex-husband's lives in danger as well as any "unlucky pedestrians" nearby.[20]

Despite Garner, Aniston, and Berry's crusade against intrusive photographers, other celebrities seem to welcome the constant attention and buzz that surround their interactions with paparazzi. Actress and reality show star Lisa Rinna commented, "Look on the positive side. There is paparazzi and there is a helicopter. You're still doing well. If there was no helicopter and no paparazzi, uh-oh time for a job."[21] Her comment was in reference to the circling photographers at her reality show co-star Denise Richards's wedding in Malibu.[22]

Paparrazo Gavin Von Karls said that his job taking photos is often at the request of celebrities: "I'm here sometimes because a celebrity told me to be here. . . . They want publicity and that's what people don't understand. Of course, there are some who absolutely do not need that publicity."[23] Musician, actor, and producer 50 Cent (a.k.a. Curtis James Jackson III) commented in a brief interview that celebrity relationships with the paparazzi are based on a fair exchange with them.[24] He said celebrities need paparazzi for the public attention to earn money to build their brand.

The Kardashian-Jenner family knows paparazzi trail them and have a symbiotic relationship with them. Von Karls believes Kim Kardashian's full-time profession is appearing on magazine covers: "This is her job too. What is she in every week? The tabloids. She doesn't act, she doesn't sing. She has a reality show but what she is in every week is the tabloids."[25] The family celebrated Kylie Jenner's nineteenth birthday at the well-known Los Angeles restaurant and paparazzi "hot spot" The Nice Guy. Many paparazzi were allowed to shoot photos inside the restaurant during the party.[26] Seemingly, there are few if any efforts by the family to restrict the paparazzi in public. The family's businesses thrive off the publicity.

In a Summer 2016 interview with *Harper's Bazaar* magazine, Kanye West (Kim Kardashian's husband) said he wanted to use the Kardashian-Jenner communication strategies to publicize a potential clothing line: "It's a lifestyle I can totally see: the future, modern Versailles, modern Versace, modern Calabasas, *paparazzi, celebrity language*. I just want to build a collection that's around me and my wife and my kids. *Because Kris and the family, they have the power of communication. This is the number-one communications company.*"[27] The power of communication that West admired earned the family the top-rated program on the E! cable network. *Keeping Up with the Kardashians* is E!'s flagship program.[28] It is a consistent top-10 unscripted reality program.[29] The Kardashian-Jenner family's communications tactics masterfully combine the television show, Instagram posts, tweets, Snapchats, *and paparazzi interactions* to increase their personal and corporate brand awareness. The paparazzi and the Kardashian-Jenners feed off one another. They give paparazzi (and entertainment press) ongoing access to their activities in return for nearly nonstop coverage.

Former *People* magazine editor Belinda Cohen says it is common practice in Hollywood for celebrities to cooperate with the paparazzi at certain times.[30] It is not unusual for publicists to inform certain paparazzi the times and locations of where a celebrity client will be. Their goal: to have the public see a specific visual that creates a narrative about the celebrity:

> You might have a celebrity who went through a break up and wants to show his or her fans that they are doing ok and are happy and they definitely want to send a message across to their ex or what have you and then they might set up a photo of them walking down the street with a big smile on their face drinking coffee.[31]

Celebrities want to control their image at all times. Cohen points out the ongoing relationships between celebrities and paparazzi. As an example, she explained the photos that appeared of Brad Pitt and Angelina Jolie on a beach in Namibia in 2006. There is no way that a paparazzo would just happen to be in Namibia at that time and take a photo. Cohen noted that Jolie is a "mastermind" of handling her image. They could have had privacy in Namibia if they wanted it. Conversely, Cohen also points to Matt Damon as an alternate example of an actor whose family has maintained a private life.[32] Between 2005 and 2012, he and his wife raised their children in semi-privacy in Miami Beach, Florida, without the paparazzi constantly following them.

CNN *Inside Man* host Morgan Spurlock spent one week shadowing paparazzi, including those who follow Kim Kardashian on a regular basis.[33] Spurlock noted that she often informs the paparazzi ahead of time about her daily travels, and they dutifully await her arrival at local restaurants or the airport when she flies home to Los Angeles.[34] For example, he explained it was really not a surprise that photographers would surround and crowd Kardashian at the Los Angeles International Airport. In the same episode, Spurlock followed fifteen photographers as they waited outside Reese Witherspoon's home for a photo. He even worked with one paparazzo who snapped an image of actor Ray Liotta working out at a local Los Angeles gym.[35]

It can be argued that celebrity culture in the United States and namely in and around Los Angeles inherently includes paparazzi activities. We need paparazzi to satisfy our desire for celebrity gossip. Consumers of celebrity magazines often say celebrity stories are a "guilty pleasure" and that "juicy gossip never hurt anyone."[36] Freelance photographers play a role in this three-billion-dollar industry since they earn money to obtain images of entertainers, the public figures whose job is to feed the public's never-ending appetite for gossip about their lives.[37] Actors, musicians, and so-called reality television stars are not immune. As long as there is an audience for the E!, *US Weekly, People,* and *InTouch* magazines and the numerous websites that post celebrity photos, paparazzi will stalk celebrities. Our cultural demand to peek inside the life of a Britney Spears or a Jennifer Aniston feeds the paparazzi frenzy.

WHO IS A CELEBRITY?

At a 1968 art exhibit in Stockholm, Sweden, Andy Warhol wrote in the exhibit's program, "In the future, everyone will be world-famous for fifteen minutes."[38] In the age of reality television, anyone who successfully auditions for a television program seems to get their fifteen minutes of fame or even longer. In 1961 historian and social theorist Daniel Boorstin defined a celebrity as a "person who is well known for his well-knownness."[39] Perhaps more pointedly for many of today's stars, "Some are born great, some achieve greatness, and some hire public relations officers."[40] Ask a group of people to define *celebrity* and you are likely to hear it is a "person famous for being famous."

For purposes of this book, the definition of *celebrity* is more specific than Boorstin's. *A celebrity is defined as someone who desires to be in the public arena achieving fame in their field.* This does not mean someone who is infamous is *not* a celebrity. But most of the people the paparazzi want to take photos of desire to achieve positive recognition in their field. Celebrities can be actors, athletes, film or television directors, producers, reality stars, authors, playwrights, and chefs. Essentially, anyone who has successfully entered the public eye for a professional accomplishment can become a celebrity. As Matthew Lee pointed out in 2015, many people in our society actively pursue celebrity status and understand that paparazzi will play a role in their lives.[41] This is why the definition of *celebrity* must include the phrase, *desires to be in the public arena.*

This by no means completely defines and identifies every celebrity, but for paparazzi these are the individuals whose photos have monetary value. Graeme Turner in 2014 explained that there are two key factors involved in the heightened marketplace of celebrity images: more paparazzi looking for images and the increasing numbers of websites that show celebrity photos.[42] These two factors are directly linked.[43] The celebrity definition that includes *public arena* reflects the multitude of online publications that publish photos.

There are many ways a person can achieve and maintain celebrity status. Many celebrities have worked in multiple entertainment fields. For example, Ron Howard starred on the *Andy Griffith Show* in the 1960s, *American Graffiti* and *Happy Days* in the 1970s, and then pursued movie directing. He won an Academy Award for directing *A Beautiful Mind.* Howard's successful work in front of and behind the camera make him a celebrity. Dwayne Johnson started his career as a professional wrestler with World Wrestling Entertainment. He transitioned to film in 2001 with his role as the Scorpion King in *The Mummy Returns*. He is now among the highest-paid movie stars and produces many Hollywood projects. The late Stan Lee, creator of Marvel Comics, was a celebrity in his own right both for creating the Spiderman, Fantastic Four, and Iron Man comic book characters, but he also wrote several television shows based on his Marvel characters and had a cameo in every Marvel movie until his death in 2019. *Wonder Woman's* Gal Gadot is a celebrity from her work as a model and an actress and she serves as a producer for the *Wonder Woman 1984* movie. *Real Housewives of Atlanta* star Nene Leakes gained her celebrity status on the reality show beginning in 2008, appeared on the FOX show *Glee* several times between 2012 and 2015, and starred on NBC's *New Normal* in 2012–2013.

Once someone has achieved celebrity status, there is an entire professional field that works to keep them in the public eye. Rein, Kotler, Hamlin, and Stoller pointed out in 2006 that the celebrity industry is supported by smaller ones, including the mass media (newspapers, magazines, television, and the Internet) along with the publicists and public relations professionals who get paid to keep individuals in the public eye.[44] Christopher Cook, a professor at Gresham College in London, explained that media, celebrities, and the public are part of an overall professional relationship.[45] Both the media and celebrities need each other in order to communicate with the public at large. Once that three-part relationship starts, it does not end: "If we reconstruct the relationship between Celebrity, Media and Consumer as a triangle rather than a straight line, then we can see that rather like nuclear fission once the process has begun it doesn't stop."[46]

As this book will discuss, many celebrities say they are violated by paparazzi who go to great lengths to get photographs and videos. As many photographers and legal experts argued, Cook sees a double standard with celebrities who demand privacy but who also want publicity for their careers: "The canny celebrity, or his or her 'people,' drip feed the media with revelation while all the while protesting at intrusion and demanding concealment."[47] Essentially, once an individual achieves that celebrity status, their lives change. Expectations of privacy change as well. Their professional careers are viewed by the public and, fair or not, includes the professional and private ups and downs of their lives.

Reality television has created a unique kind of celebrity. As Choi and Berger noted in 2009, "Reality TV makes people famous for being themselves."[48] They state that there is a lot of room in the media for many to achieve celebrity status.[49] The field interviews conducted for this book often included a discussion of reality television stars and their claim to fame. Paparazzo Giles Harrison, in an interview, stated that many reality television shows make us care about the mundane, everyday lives of the cast and he cannot quite understand why.[50] He noted that once that celebrity status is achieved, a photo of someone such as reality stars Tamra Judge or Mercedes Javid is now worth money. That financial value does not originate from scripted projects, just from an average person's desire to be famous.

Reality television has also relaunched careers. Denise Richards, Lisa Rinna, and Kandi Burrus have all experienced a new wave of success in recent years. Richards was a model and television and movie actress, Rinna a soap opera star on *Days of Our Lives*, and Burrus an award-winning song writer and singer. The reality genre also gives others a way to promote their other businesses. For example, Lisa Vanderpump uses the *Real Housewives of Beverly Hills* and *Vanderpump Rules* to promote her restaurants and dog rescue foundation. Josh Flagg appears on *Million Dollar Listing* and can generate real estate business from that show. The Kardashian–Jenner family uses its reality shows to showcase their businesses: clothing, makeup, and skin care products. Unlike the traditional means to stardom through acting or athletic talent, reality television creates celebrities who, in turn, promote their other businesses or philanthropic causes.

Since this book focuses on whether California's anti-paparazzi laws have impacted the photographers' professions, anyone considered a noteworthy public figure by the photographers is considered a celebrity. In Los Angeles, the epicenter of the entertainment industry, those people are actors, directors, producers, athletes, reality stars, etc. If the paparazzi are actively seeking them out for photos or act upon a tip to find and photograph them, then they are celebrities.

CELEBRITY COMPLAINTS ABOUT PAPARAZZI

When paparazzi overstep and stake out celebrities' homes or follow them around town, many celebrities openly cry foul. Some take it a step further. Several, including Justin Bieber, Alec Baldwin, and Lamar Odom, have had noted physical altercations with photographers. There are numerous examples where celebrities have taken to television, newspapers, and social media to plead for privacy. Kristen Bell and her husband, Dax Shepard actively pointed out how paparazzi were following them and their newborn daughter.[51] Bell used Twitter to amplify her complaint by calling them "hunters" and "predators."[52] She staked out a First Amendment freedom of press argument against paparazzi by retweeting a follower's support: "The Founding Fathers could never've anticipated such misuse of the #FirstAmendment. #PhotographersGoneWild #pedorazzi."[53]

Bell and Shepard also launched the Twitter campaign, #NoKidsPolicy, a successful initiative that asked media not to publish children's photos unless it had permission of the parents.[54] They obtained a promise of cooperation from several media shows and outlets: *Entertainment Tonight, Access Hollywood, Extra, E! Entertainment, Inside Edition, US Weekly, Entertainment Weekly, Reuters, Associated Press,* and *People* magazine.[55] Bell and Shepard received support from other celebrities: Bradley Cooper, Ellen DeGeneres, Amy Poehler, Ben Affleck, Amy Adams, and Scarlett Johansson.[56] In 2016 actress Hilary Duff used the #NoKidsPolicy Twitter hashtags to ask the press to stop publishing photos of her son Luca.[57]

Even Khloe Kardashian at one time had her fill of paparazzi activity. In May 2015, she tweeted her frustrations after she and her mother, Kris Jenner, and sister Kendall Jenner were crowded by photographers when exiting a Los Angeles store: "Paparazzi need to understand that if they keep violating rules & private property laws then we will take action. Play nice & so will we."[58] Singer Demi Lovato in June 2016 tweeted that our cultural obsession with celebrities fueled the paparazzi: "I bet our country knows more about celebrities than they know about what's happening over seas or global warming."[59] She then correctly noted the hypocrisy between public dislike for paparazzi and our cultural obsession with celebrity gossip: "We complain about how unfair paparazzi and tabloid rumors are but still buy the magazines to find out who's fucking who and who wore it best."[60]

In attempt to offer support for celebrities in the pushback against the paparazzi, former celebrity bodyguard Sean Burke founded the Paparazzi Reform Initiative in 2009. It is a California-based organization that seeks to limit paparazzi conduct in the name of privacy. Its mission is: "The restoration of an individual's right to privacy in our rapidly advancing technological age through education, legal action, lobbying and other effective methods."[61] As an advocacy organization, the Paparazzi Reform Initiative has fought for tighter privacy laws in California, including the 2014 laws discussed in chapter 3.

ARE THE PAPARAZZI PROTECTED BY THE FIRST AMENDMENT?

Tabloid magazines, websites, and television shows obtain many of their photos and videos from paparazzi. They are the field-based photographers and videographers who either work full-time for a TMZ type of media organization or sell their images on a freelance basis to a photo agency that, in turn, sells to magazines and websites. They are the ones who help feed our society's appetite for celebrity news. Paparazzo Giles Harrison argued the freedom of press perspective: "We are journalists and just because you don't like the subject matter, you can't blame the paparazzi for capitalizing on it. I understand the inherent annoyance that comes from celebrities toward us, but then unfortunately that's the kind of the price you pay."[62] Harrison reminds us that the lack of privacy for celebrities is consumer driven. The magazine editors buy his photos because consumers purchase the magazines; it is a cyclical business relationship.[63]

In her summer 2016 *Huffington Post* blog post, Jennifer Aniston wrote: "For the record, I am not pregnant. What I am is fed up. I'm fed up with the sport-like scrutiny and body shaming that occurs daily under the guise of 'journalism,' the 'First Amendment' and 'celebrity news.'"[64] Aniston leads us to believe that she does not think that paparazzi (and tabloid) activities on celebrities are conducted as credible journalism within the First Amendment. Her placing the terms *journalism* and *First Amendment* in quotation marks could lead any reader to this conclusion. While she may be justified in her opinion of the horde of photographers who follow her every move, legally she is incorrect. For better or worse, the paparazzi and their mass media clients are considered press under U.S. law and entitled to legal rights.

Aniston is not alone in her assessment. Kris Herzog, the owner of the Bodyguard Group of Beverly Hills, says celebrities should argue, "We're not leaving until you a pass a constitutional amendment that says freedom of the press does not apply to paparazzi. It only applies to people not breaking the law, harassment is breaking the law, not trespassing on private property and not interfering in the private lives of public people."[65] Herzog likens paparazzi to stalkers who use their cameras instead of weapons. But unlike stalkers, they are protected by the First Amendment's freedom of press guarantee. He believes their only goal is "making a buck" in entertainment.[66] His argument is that a stalker is just as dangerous with a camera as with a weapon. To counter that perspective, paparazzo Giles Harrison argued that California has had anti-stalking, harassment, and trespassing laws and did not need any more laws to restrict paparazzi activities.[67]

First Amendment jurisprudence recognizes different forms of media from the traditional newspaper, to broadcast radio and television, to the Internet. This includes the paparazzi employed by these news outlets either in full-time or freelance capacities. In the digital communications era of the Internet, photographers and private bloggers are citizen media activists entitled to First Amendment free speech and press rights. Unlike doctors, attorneys, and accountants, reporters and photographers are not licensed professionals in the United States. Anyone can claim to be a part of the media. In this country, no state or federal license is needed to open a news media operation. The First Amendment free speech and press provisions do not require any professional operating license.

In the twenty-first century, many paparazzi photos and videos are posted on numerous websites such as TMZ.com, people.com, and perezhilton.com. Paparazzo Giles Harrison remarked that in the digital age, "The Internet is so accessible, all these images are bombarded at us every day."[68] The use of the Internet as a media platform for celebrity images is protected under the First Amendment. In 1997 in *Reno v. ACLU*, Justice John Paul Stevens wrote the Supreme Court's landmark opinion that the Internet is a legally protected speech platform for disseminating all types of information:

> Any person or organization with a computer connected to the Internet can "publish" information. Publishers include government agencies, educational institutions, commercial entities, advocacy groups, and individuals. Publishers may either make their material available to the entire pool of Internet users, or confine access to a selected group, such as those willing to pay for the privilege.[69]

The Court's opinion in *Reno v. ACLU* clearly shows that the Internet is available to anyone who wishes to use it including paparazzi, celebrity media companies, and celebrities themselves. As previously discussed, the Kardashian-Jenner family uses tools of the Internet in the form of Instagram and Twitter to publish photos and videos for their followers. Paparazzi and media companies do likewise.

Most states in the United States have shield laws that protect the media from disclosing confidential sources in front of a state grand jury under certain circumstances. These laws often include language that defines *who* under state law is protected media and what their legal rights are when protecting confidential sources. Essentially, states—including California—have laws that provide a definition for journalists and the media they work for. These designations could be applied to journalists and the media. According to the Society of Professional Journalists, forty-nine states have shield laws that often include definitions of journalists and specifically paparazzi.[70] Three of those states are the primary locations for television, film, and music industries and where celebrities have homes: California, New York, and Georgia. For example in California (home to most paparazzi), the shield law in the state's Constitution recognizes media personnel as "A publisher, editor, reporter, or other person connected with or employed upon a newspaper, magazine, or other periodical publication, or by a press association or wire service, or any person who has been so connected or employed."[71] In 2006 in *O'Grady vs. Superior Court*, a state appeals court ruled that the entire shield law, including the definition of journalists, included online publications.[72] Under California state law, paparazzi who freelance for traditional and online media outlets may be within their rights to photograph celebrities at all times unless they violate state privacy, harassment, or trespassing laws.

Some state shield laws provide specific definitions of journalists that could include paparazzi photographers. For example, New York's shield law contains explicit language describing not only who is considered a journalist but what constitutes a news organization.[73] A newspaper, magazine, news agency, press association, and wire service are all defined under New York law.[74] Under the law, paparazzi may be considered a "professional journalist" since they gather video images and photographs. The term "journalist" applies to a full-time employee of a media organization or a *freelance photographer* or videographer who is "professionally affiliated" with an organization and receives pay for content.[75] Section 8 of the law defines news as: "written, oral, pictorial, *photo-*

graphic, or electronically recorded information or communication concerning local, national or worldwide events or other matters of public concern or public interest or affecting the public welfare."[76]

While California and New York are two states that have specific parameters about what journalists do professionally, in Georgia the state's shield law does not provide a definition of journalist, but instead focuses on types of media organizations: "Any person, company, or other entity engaged in the gathering and dissemination of news for the public through any newspaper, book, magazine, radio or television broadcast, or electronic means."[77] The statute does not include a definition for news. Local paparazzi may not have as much legal protection under Georgia's law as they do in California or New York, but they still have a fundamental right to work in their profession.

Both the First Amendment and state shield laws recognize a wide variety of media in the country. This does not mean the media has an *absolute* right to free press. State anti-stalking and invasion of privacy laws apply to the media as much as to any individual. In 2014 California passed two laws aimed at the paparazzi based on invasion of privacy and stalking.[78] Chapter 3 discusses these restrictions and how California has attempted to use privacy and stalking laws to limit the paparazzi.

NOTES

1. Jennifer Aniston, "For the Record," *Huffington Post*, July 12, 2016.
2. Tina Daunt, "Jennifer Garner Joins Halle Berry in Fight for Tougher Anti-Parazzi Law," *The Hollywood Reporter*, August 14, 2013, http://www.hollywoodreporter.com/news/jennifer-garner-joins-halle-berry-60641.
3. Ibid.
4. Katherine Lam, "Scarlett Johansson Taken to Los Angeles Police Station Following Paparazzi Incident," FOXNews.com, April 9, 2019, https://www.foxnews.com/entertainment/scarlett-johansson-taken-to-los-angeles-police-station-following-paparazzi-incident.
5. Ibid.
6. Eriq Gardner, "California Law Punishing Paparazzi for High-Speed Celebrity Chases Is Upheld," *The Hollywood Reporter*, September 30, 2015, http://www.hollywoodreporter.com/thr-esq/california-law-punishing-paparazzi-high-828437.
7. Carol Squiers, "Class Struggle: The Invention of Paparazzi Photography and the Death of Diana, Princess of Wales," in *Overexposed: Essay on Contemporary Photography*, ed. Carol Squiers (New York, NY: The Press, 1999), 269.
8. Ibid., 289.
9. Cal. Veh. Code §40008 (2015).
10. Carol Squiers, "Original Sin: The Birth of the Paparazzo," in Exposed: Voyeurism, Surveillance, and the Camera since 1870," ed. Sandra Phillips (San Francisco, CA: San Francisco Museum of Modern Art, 2010), 221.
11. Kim McNamara, *Paparazzi: Media Practices and Celebrity Culture* (Malden, MA: Polity Press, 2016) 41.
12. Eriq Gardner, "California Law Punishing Paparazzi."
13. *Raef v. Appellate Division of the Superior County of Los Angeles*, 240 Cal. App. 4th 1121 (2015).

14. Nicholas Schmidle, "The Digital Dirt: How TMZ Gets the Videos and Photos that Celebrities Want to Hide," *The New Yorker*, February 22, 2013, http://www.newyorker.com/magazine/2016/02/22/inside-harvey-levins-tmz.
15. Ibid.
16. Ibid.
17. "The Paparazzi Industry," *The Paparazzi Reform Initiative*, http://www.paparazzi-reform.org/industry/.
18. Reuters, "California bill protecting children of celebrities from paparazzi signed into law," *Daily News*, September 25, 2013, http://www.nydailynews.com/news/national/halle-berry-jennifer-garner-supported-california-bill-protecting-children-paparazzi-signed-law-article-1.1467192.
19. Jennifer Aniston, "The Blog: For the Record," *Huffington Post*, July 12, 2016, http://www.huffingtonpost.com/entry/for-the-record_us_57855586e4b03fc3ee4e626f.
20. Ibid.
21. "Eat, Drink and Be Married," an episode in *Real Housewives of Beverly Hills*.
22. Ibid. Denise Richards married Aaron Phypers on September 8, 2018.
23. "Celebrity," an episode in *Morgan Spurlock, Inside Man*.
24. Interview with 50 Cent, June 17, 2019.
25. Ibid.
26. Ali Szubiak, "Kylie Jenner Celebrates 19th Birthday a Full 10 Days Early," *Pop Crush*, August 1, 2016, http://popcrush.com/kylie-jenner-19-birthday-party/.
27. Carine Roitfeld, "Icons: In Bed with Kim and Kanye," *Harpers Bazaar*, July 28, 2016, http://www.harpersbazaar.com/fashion/photography/a16784/kanye-west-kim-kardashian-interview/. Author's italicization of quotation.
28. Rick Kissell, "3-Day Ratings: 'Survivor,' 'Keeping Up With the Kardashians' Still Going Strong," *Variety*, May 6, 2016, http://variety.com/2016/tv/news/3-day-ratings-survivor-keeping-up-with-the-kardashians-1201768322/.
29. Ibid.
30. Belinda Cohen, [psued.] (former editor, *People* magazine) in discussion with author, March 2018.
31. Ibid.
32. Ibid.
33. "Celebrity," an episode in *Morgan Spurlock, Inside Man*.
34. Ibid.
35. Ibid.
36. Ibid.
37. Ibid.
38. Modern Museet, Stockholm, Sweden, 1968.
39. Daniel Boorstin, *The Image: A Guide to Pseudo-Events in America* (New York: Vintage 1961).
40. Ibid.
41. Matthew Lee, "Strict Liability and the Anti-Paparazzi Act: The Best Solution to Protect Children of Celebrities," *Hastings Law Journal*, Vol. 66 (2015): 7.
42. Graeme Turner, "Is celebrity news, news?" *Journalism*, Vol. 15, no. 2 (2014), 146.
43. Ibid.
44. Irving Rein, Philip Kotler, Michael Hamlin, and Martin Stoller, *High Visibility: Transforming Your Personal and Professional Brand* (New York: McGraw Hill, 2006).
45. Christopher Cook, "The Making of Modern Celebrity: Famous for Fifteen Minutes—and Longer" (presentation, Gresham College Lecture, London, UK Wednesday, February 9, 2011).
46. Ibid.
47. Ibid.
48. Chong Ju Choi and Ron Berger, "Ethics of Celebrities and Their Increasing Influence in 21st Century Society," *Journal of Business Ethics*, Vol. 91 (2010): 316.
49. Ibid.
50. Interview with Paparazzo Giles Harrison, July 15, 2019.

51. Kristen Bell's uses the Twitter handle @IMKristenBell and Dax Shepard's Twitter handle is @daxshepard1. In 2014 they launched a series of Twitter hashtags including #FirstAmendment. #PhotographersGoneWild #pedorazzi in their desire to limit paparazzi intrusion into celebrities' children's lives.
52. Maria Puente, "Celebs push back against the paparazzi," *USA Today*, March 28, 2014, http://www.usatoday.com/story/life/people/2014/03/22/celebs-push-back-against-the-paparazzi/6186163/.
53. Ibid.
54. Ibid.
55. Ibid.
56. Ibid.
57. Hilary Duff's Twitter handles are @HilaryDuff and @HilaryNews. In 2016 she posted several photos of her and young son Luca taken by various paparazzi using the hashtag #NoKidsPolicy urging them to respect her family's privacy.
58. Teresa Roca, "Watch What Forced Kloe Kardashian to Fire at the Paparazzi After Shopping Trip with Kris and Kendall Jenner," *OK!*, May 12, 2015, http://okmagazine.com/videos/khloe-kardashian-fires-paparazzi-shopping-trip-kendall-jenner-kris-jenner/.
59. Kathleen Wong, "Demi Lovato Returns to Social Media and Calls Out People's Celebrity Obsessions," *Music.Mic*, June 24, 2016, https://mic.com/articles/147035/demi-lovato-returns-to-social-media-and-calls-out-people-s-celebrity-obsessions#.JJu4RuNnU.
60. Ibid.
61. "Mission Statement," Paparazzi Reform Initiative, 2016, http://www.paparazzireform.org/about/mission-statement/.
62. "Celebrity," an episode in *Morgan Spurlock, Inside Man*.
63. Ibid.
64. Jennifer Aniston, "The Blog: For the Record," *Huffington Post*, July 12, 2016, http://www.huffingtonpost.com/entry/for-the-record_us_57855586e4b03fc3ee4e626f.
65. "Celebrity," an episode in *Morgan Spurlock, Inside Man*.
66. Ibid.
67. Giles Harrison (paparazzo) in discussion with author, April 2018.
68. Ibid.
69. 521 U.S. 844 (1997), 843.
70. Society of Professional Journalists, "Shield Law 101: Frequently Asked Questions," http://www.spj.org/shieldlaw-faq.asp.
71. Cal. Const. Art. 1 §2(b).
72. Cal. Ct. App. (2006).
73. New York Civil Rights Law § 79-h (a)(3)(2016).
74. New York Civil Rights Law § 79-h (2016).
75. New York Civil Rights Law § 79-h (a)(6) (2016).
76. New York Civil Rights Law § 79-h (a)(8) 2016).
77. O.C.G.A. § 24-5-508 (2016).
78. Cal. Civ. Code §1708.8 (2014) and Cal. Civ. Code §1708.7 (2014).

TWO

Paparazzi as Journalists

A journalist or paparazzo? Can a photographer be both? Can a photographer be respected and scorned at the same time? Some paparazzi consider themselves to be credible photojournalists. Famed paparazzo Ron Galella considers himself a mainstream photojournalist.[1] He did not worry about how the public views his interactions with celebrities: "Stars maybe don't like it, but at the end of the day they want to see themselves in the magazines and on TV. We are considered parasites and intruders. For me, it's not true, and it doesn't affect me."[2] Galella's colleague Pascal Rostain claimed that in some countries, depending on circumstances, one day the public may consider him a paparazzo and on another day as a photojournalist. Until Princess Diana's death in 1997, he and others were comfortable in straddling the two professional categories of journalist and paparazzo. After her tragic death from the infamous highway chase in Paris, Galella and others were universally condemned as paparazzi and not celebrated as journalists.[3] Essentially, photographers who follow celebrities are now often placed into the paparazzi category.

With issues of privacy, the news value associated with celebrity-focused information is one that courts often have to decide. According to Professor Amy Gajda, when journalists need to make a decision about a story that could invade someone's privacy, they may often look to their professional ethics code for guidelines.[4] Ethics can help the photographer make difficult decisions. For example, a paparazzo may pay someone to tip them off for a celebrity's location whereas most reporters will not violate their professional ethics and exchange money for access opportunity.[5] State laws may recognize that *newsworthy* stories that impact the public have more legal protection when it comes to allegations of invasion of privacy than those stories or photos that are deemed sensational.[6] Fair or not, a courtroom judge often determines whether the materials in question are important enough to be broadcast or published. Therefore, the judge determines whether or not there is a news value for the public to receive the information.

Some paparazzi photos and videos may be seen as "quasi-journalism" since this content is often published outside of mainstream news outlets.[7] These photos may contain personal information about a celebrity. Photographers and publishers may or may not include the ethical considerations discussed later in this chapter. It is essentially a gray line of journalism that falls somewhere between traditional journalism and the paparazzi materials that are sourced from their questionable actions.

Professor Graeme Turner wrote in 2014 that traditional celebrity news can be defined as the reporting and commentary about celebrities' lives.[8] Unlike hard news, celebrity or entertainment reporting is not as objective in its reporting and writing. A lot of celebrity-focused news is generated by the celebrities themselves through their manager and publicity firm.[9] Turner noted that celebrity news differs from traditional hard news since it has more of a commercial purpose to it.[10] That commercial purpose is drumming up information, "news" about the celebrity or event. That news may be about a new romantic relationship, fashion style, or recent travel. The matter in which information is conveyed regarding a celebrity is quite different than how hard news is covered.

With a breaking hard news story, a reporter may be told through a press release or last-minute telephone call to attend an event or visit a crime scene to interview the relevant people. Hard news is often not planned ahead of time. As Turner noted, celebrity news, on the other hand, is "provided to journalists via press releases, press packs, access to events, through personal contact with the publicity and promotion organizations generating interest in new commercial vehicles . . . or through the publicity arm of the celebrity's own management team."[11] Essentially, in the world of entertainment, the information is nearly *spoon-fed* to the reporter. Conversely, in hard news, the reporter often takes the lead in seeking out information about the story and finding the relevant people to interview.

While celebrity-based journalism is different than hard news, in its own right, it is different than what paparazzi do on a daily basis. Celebrity news journalists are a "filtering agent" they sort out what are often multiple offers to attend parties, movie premieres, and charity events sponsored by celebrities and their publicists.[12] The free publicity for the celebrity occurs if and when a reporter attends the invited event. Journalists often attend these events as a means of keeping contact with the different publicists and agents. According to Turner, many of them are aware that they participate in turning personal "advertising into news."[13] The celebrity promotes an activity, and the journalist uses that information for a story. Turner noted the relationship between journalist and publicist or celebrity is symbiotic. The reporter needs the publicist for articles on their entertainment beat, and the publicist needs the reporter to advertise and promote their client, the celebrity.[14] Both parties know they need each other to be successful. Red carpet events or movie premieres are examples of mainstream celebrity news.

Unlike the symbiotic relationship between the celebrity and the reporter, paparazzi have unique approaches to their jobs. As Kevin Frazier, co-host of *Entertainment Tonight* and founder of hiphollywood.com, explains, there are actually two types of paparazzi.[15] The first are those who freelance for different photo agencies and are invited to attend red carpet events and premieres. They are physically placed in one area and continuously take photos as each celebrity walks by. These paparazzi attend the red carpet events and premieres with the required media credentials for those events. On those occasions, the paparazzi are categorized as mainstream press. Their job is to capture photos and video of the event so that it is publicized in the media. According to Frazier, the second group of paparazzi are the ones who often follow celebrities who are out and about in Los Angeles. They drive around the city, wait for them at the airport, and pay restaurant and hotel staff to call them with a tip about the celebrity's locations.[16] This second group of paparazzi are the ones whose actions often demean all paparazzi. Vince Flores, a photographer who worked as both types of paparazzi, would be issued press credentials to an event and then after it finished, would drive around Los Angeles looking for celebrities to photograph.[17]

Kevin Frazier is not alone in differentiating between the two groups of paparazzi who exist in California. *L.A.Times* celebrity reporter Christie D'Zurilla noted that the two groups of paparazzi have different techniques:

> There are people just trying to get a picture and get the picture that nobody else has so they can sell it for a whole bunch of money. That's the more traditional paparazzo definition where it's just straight photography. Am I going to get the picture of Britney Spears shaving her head? Am I going to get the best picture of Michael Jackson's kids coming out of the Cirque du Soleil show that was about him. There's another kind of video journalist that gets lumped in with the paparazzi and that's the TMZ style video interviewer where those people are trying to ask questions. . . . They are trying to get video clips, some news out of it.[18]

Most bystanders do not notice this difference in the two groups of Los Angeles paparazzi. According to D'Zurilla, the lines between the two can often get blurry:

> When the photographers are working the red carpet say at the Vanity Fair after-party . . . at that point they start out at assigned positions on the bleachers spread out along the red carpet and a couple of hours later are all crammed into about 20 percent of the space at the far end

> because they all kind of scooted and scooted so they become sort of that mob, that photography mob but they are all technically legitimate journalists from respected outlets.[19]

Regardless of which group of paparazzi any photographer may be associated with, according to Kevin Frazier, their mission is essentially the same, getting the *one-of-a-kind* photograph of a celebrity that will be published in the printed magazines and posted online soon after the event: "It was just all about getting into place to get the shot. So, you will get a lot of guys who maybe wouldn't be employed otherwise or in other situations but they are employed because they can chase down and get that shot."[20] Frazier noted that essentially, it comes down to just one main goal: "To get in front of that celebrity and click with their cameras. Get in front of that celebrity and get the shot."[21]

That jockeying for position does not just exist at the red carpet events and premieres, but is a staple for those California paparazzi who wait outside restaurants to take photos. Getty Images, 20th Century FOX, and Instar Images freelance photographer Sam Kelogg has friends who are paparazzi who often elbow for that best position to take *the* photograph outside any well-regarded celebrity restaurant in Los Angeles: "Some are, when a celebrity comes out of a night club, there's shoving and pushing and stuff. They are kind of like gang members because you have to be rough to do that because you get shoved around a lot, you have to be aggressive."[22]

As paparazzi compete with one another for celebrities' images, there is an emerging subject pattern to their photos. In a 2013 study of paparazzi subjects, Jerslev and Mortensen found that 93 percent of all their photos detailed celebrities in "everyday situations" with their family or running errands.[23] Very few photos, 7 percent, were images of celebrities in potentially embarrassing situations where they were inebriated, arrested, or partially clothed.[24] Jersley and Mortensen discovered that 40 percent of all photos are the day-to-day activities of celebrities while 37 percent of photos are from red carpet events.[25] Photos of daily, ordinary activities do not have the celebrity posing for the camera, whereas the red carpet photos are the one with celebrities posing. Jerslev and Mortensen learned there is an overabundance of celebrity images on the internet, but those same photos do not reveal any surprising information about the celebrity subject.[26]

As an industry, paparazzi photography is a "rough-edged hybrid" of several forms of photography: photojournalism, documentary, celebrity-focused, and surveillance.[27] The images are photojournalistic in style when news is conveyed about a celebrity. Professor and photography editor Carol Squiers and paparazzo Ron Galella both believe that paparazzi photography can have a news value.[28] Yet, Squiers also explained that in most cases the paparazzi use these various forms of photography in a way "that maximizes outrage and seems to blanket the entire medium in disgrace."[29] An example of celebrity images with news value is the wedding of a celebrity couple such as Prince Harry and Meghan Markle in 2018 or celebrities who volunteer at a charity event such as Kate Hudson appearing at the annual Watch Hunger Stop event.[30] Squiers noted the documentary style of photography occurs when images record a "reality" of celebrity life.[31] Still images from the 2014 Netflix documentary *Mitt* about Mitt Romney, the former presidential candidate and now Utah senator is an example, as well as 2014's HBO's *Beyoncé: Life Is But a Dream*. Instead of producing these kinds of informative documentaries, paparazzi, according to Squiers, would produce a series of photos focusing on celebrities' wealth and privilege.[32] Their documentary-like approach would focus on the celebrities' private daily routines (driving, shopping, eating, child care) or when they are on vacation, often at destinations most of us cannot afford.

Celebrity-focused photography is often when celebrities and their publicists release images used by celebrity magazines and websites.[33] Surveillance photography conducted by paparazzi are those photos that aim to capture the possible illegal or immoral acts of celebrities that are also embarrassing.[34] The act of surveillance photography parallels one of the goals of the California anti-paparazzi laws discussed in chapter 3, preventing paparazzi from continuously following celebrity subjects and invading their privacy. Under Section 1708.8 of the state Civil Code, it is illegal to harass celebrities or follow them surreptitiously and invade their privacy to capture private moments.[35]

ENTERTAINMENT JOURNALIST VS. PAPARAZZO

While many paparazzi including Ron Galella believe they are professional photojournalists, a major question is how mainstream entertainment journalists view the paparazzi since they often write and produce stories about the same celebrities. Many of these celebrity journalists indicate some form of admiration for the paparazzi work ethic and how they doggedly pursue their subjects. Award-winning photojournalist Dave Burnett is one those members of the press who appreciates the voluminous amounts of time paparazzi put into their jobs:

> When I see these guys at the LA airport and there always a few of these guys and hanging out and I'm like man it's kind of a lousy way to make a buck but the thing is there is a gigantic market for it and appetite for it that I guess it's a little like drugs.[36]

In 2017 Burnett was named by *American Photo* magazine as one of the top 100 most important people in photography. He was also honored in 2018 with the Sprague Award for Lifetime Achievement by the National Press

Photographers Association. While Burnett does not consider paparazzi as his peers, he does respect the work they do:

> There is this sense of how people are able to go into very difficult situations and make good pictures. Some of these guys are incredibly good photographers and you can say in a way it's a waste of good work . . . just from a technical point of view, the ability to pull off the stuff they get. I'm kind of wow that is amazing.[37]

L.A. Times entertainment reporter Christie D'Zurilla admires how hard California paparazzi work. She sees them in action at dozens of red-carpet events.[38] She also respects the *TMZ*-style reporter who uses traditional reporting methods to interview celebrities rather than stalk them on the street: "You have either one person interviewing and another person running the camera with the person on the camera asking the questions. They are trying to get video clips, some news out of it. But to me that has a little more substance."[39] Essentially, TMZ field producers seek video soundbites, whereas photographers take the still image. Entertainment journalists such as D'Zurilla, Burnett, Kevin Frazier, and Sam Kelogg all agree that when the paparazzi go to extremes and chase after the celebrity in their cars, or in extreme cases pick through their trash or climb fences, they lose credibility among the public and from many of their paparazzi peers. Those actions give the industry its bad reputation.

Despite the tarnished reputations and perceived lack of ethics, many entertainment reporters believe in the First Amendment's guarantees of free speech and press protect the paparazzi and the profession. Photojournalist Dave Burnett compares the paparazzi's reputation to that of *Penthouse* publisher Larry Flynt:

> There was this whole thing twenty years ago when Larry Flynt ended up being the great defender of the First Amendment and everybody was like 'Oh my God, why does it have to be Larry Flynt?' The thing about freedom of the press is the more annoying it is to you, those are the kind of people who need to be protected the most.[40]

Journalists such as Burnett believe the First Amendment applies as much to the paparazzi profession as it does to him. Echoing the words of Burnett, D'Zurillo points out the First Amendment applies to all photographers and it is not bound by ethical considerations of anyone's profession: "In many ways I don't think they are an overall positive in society, but does the Constitution care? I don't think so."[41]

Burnett has little sympathy for celebrities who complain about intrusion into their lives but at the same time seek the public's attention. He argues they cannot have it "both ways" in complaining about the paparazzi taking their photos at inconvenient moments but then embrace other media when it is convenient for them.[42] By placing themselves in the public eye, celebrities have no choice but to balance the public image they want to portray with their private lives:

> It becomes a phony argument when you have one week they are working on trying to get out their next PR campaign and then the week after that they are trying to get everything shut down because they want to be able to go to Spago and not be followed. So, I have to say it's a pretty dull line, it's not a sharp line.[43]

Attorney and Director of the Brechner Center for Freedom of Information, Frank LoMonte says without doubt paparazzi work is protected by the First Amendment freedom of press. He noted that if paparazzi sell photographs to a publication that informs people of lifestyles and activities of celebrities, then that is a form of journalism.[44] It is that simple. LoMonte said that the issue of free press activity is a little more complicated if the sole purpose of a paparazzo is to post photos on a website where anyone can purchase and download them as if they are souvenirs. In that case, First Amendment press protection may no longer apply.[45] He stated the paparazzo's photography is then a purely commercial act and celebrities' permission may be needed for that commercial function. In this scenario, the celebrity has commercial rights to how their images are sold. The sole news function of the paparazzo telling a story within the image may no longer exist. Yet, if the paparazzi are taking photos to tell an entertainment oriented news story, then, according to LoMonte, their actions are a form of journalism.

JOURNALISM ETHICS

Most mainstream journalists, including photographers and videographers, adhere to a code of ethics. Several journalism organizations provide ethics standards on how to treat subjects of a news story including those subjects who are photographed or recorded by video. Newsrooms across various media platforms incorporate some or all of these ethical precepts. The professional ethics described below emphasize how to treat people who are interviewed, photographed, or recorded on video. In all these ethics codes, *respect* is at the core of how subjects should be treated.

One of the principles the Society of Professional Journalists (SPJ) espouses is *minimizing* harm. Specifically, the second section of SPJ's Code of Ethics states, "Ethical journalism treats sources, subjects, colleagues and members of the public as human beings deserving of respect."[46] SPJ encourages its members to show compassion for the people they interview and avoid "pandering to curiosity."[47] It can be argued that paparazzi actually supply the product for the public's demand of these images by appealing to the public's curiosity. A major part of SPJ's ethical approach is that the "pursuit of news is not a license for arrogance or undue intrusiveness."[48]

SPJ is not alone in its ethics approach to avoid harming the subjects of a story. The Radio Television Digital News Association (RTDNA) includes references in its ethical standards to avoid deceptive news gathering.[49] "Surreptitious recording" conflicts with journalism's goal in obtaining the truth in any story.[50] Many paparazzi often employ deceptive news-gathering techniques such as the use of high-powered telephoto lenses or paying informants for celebrity locations in and around Los Angeles. In the age of social media, RTDNA encourages accuracy over the need to post a story online quickly for it to go viral or trend on social media.[51] This is in direct opposition to one of the paparazzi's professional goals: quickly selling their images for publication.

One organization focused on visual journalism is the National Press Photographer's Association (NPPA). Its code of ethics tells photographers and video journalists not to influence events in order to gain a great visual.[52] It strictly tells its members not "to engage in harassing behavior of colleagues, subordinates, or subjects."[53] Some paparazzi purposely create conflict with celebrities just to create a visualized incident that can turn into a story.

All three organizations' code of ethics focus on treating individuals with respect in the pursuit of journalism. The techniques often employed by rogue paparazzi violate most of these ethical mores. Paparazzi, at their worst, violate their subjects' privacy, harass them, sneak photos and videos, and often create an openly hostile environment for their celebrity subjects. One negative incident can poison a celebrity's future relationship with many or all paparazzi.

Journalism ethics guidelines are written for *anyone* who works full-time for a news organization or as a freelance reporter who sells stories, photographs, or videos to a general news publication or an entertainment-focused media organization. While they sell their photos to media outlets and agencies, a few paparazzi claim to have a personal ethics code. Yet, some of the most famous and well-regarded paparazzi eschew the idea of ethics in their profession. Ron Galella, who is famous for his never-ending quest to photograph Jackie Kennedy Onassis in New York City in the 1970s, stated the only ethical code he followed was based on whether celebrities slammed their front doors on him.[54] He claims that he did not pursue obtrusive methods to gain access to their home. Another well-known paparazzo, French photographer Pascal Rostain, noted, "The limits are not fixed by our profession, nor by the people we photograph, nor by the magazines we work for."[55]

French paparazzo Sébastien Valiela remarked that there is no written code of ethics that paparazzi use.[56] Their codes of ethics are based on personal beliefs. The do's and don't's for one paparazzo may not apply to another. Where one paparazzo will not photograph children or dead bodies, another may choose to do so. According to another French paparazzo, Francis Apesteguy, "It is a question of mental references."[57] California-based freelance photographer Sam Kellog said that ethics plays no role with most paparazzi in Hollywood.[58] They will take photographs of people and create a fictitious story line caption without knowing facts; hide in a car in a hospital parking garage; or even sneak onto an ambulance for a photograph of a sick or dead celebrity for the *one-in-a-million* photo, then cash in: "The other guy that got a picture of Michael Jackson's dead body in the ambulance. This guy was an idiot. He got lucky. He just ran up and put his camera to the ambulance click and he made a couple of million dollars on that. Something like that is once in a lifetime."[59] Kellog also pointed out that lying is standard in the paparazzi profession:

> One of my buddies is paparazzi. And he was waiting for Johnny Depp to show up. He [Depp] got out of the car and he kissed his publicist on the cheek. Some agency in France took that photo, conjured up a story that he was having an affair with this woman and it was all bullshit. He made 50 grand on that photo out of something that isn't even true. So, you get a photo and make something up out of it and the photographer reaps the awards of it.[60]

In addition to a lack of established ethics for paparazzi, some photographers will also endanger bystanders to obtain *the* photograph or video. For example, three paparazzi who were working for the same agency once teamed up in their individual cars to block other photographers from gaining photos of Britney Spears while she was driving on a California road.[61] This incident put drivers at risk.

The absence of ethics was clearly on display in August 1997 when Princess Diana and her boyfriend died in a car accident that started with the paparazzi chasing them at high speeds on a Paris highway.[62] That same lack of moral direction was also evident in 2012 when the paparazzi chased after Justin Bieber on Los Angeles highways, endangering both him and other drivers. Professor and philosopher Dale Jacquette remarked this is a natural result of the often chaotic relationships between celebrities and paparazzi: "Placing excessive stress on celebrities and their staff in the way that the persistent tactics of paparazzi inevitably do there will likely continue to be such terrible accidents as befell Diana and Dodi."[63] Critics such as Jacquette believe the paparazzi's main motivation is simply a big payday for the once-in-a-lifetime photograph.[64] Within the realm of entertainment journalism, the paparazzi's intrusive behavior cannot be justified.[65] Chapter 4 will discuss the personal ethics codes used by paparazzi interviewed in Los Angeles.

CONCLUSION

This chapter illustrated that the paparazzi profession is complicated, as it can be described an edgy form of journalism or as an intrusion into celebrities' private lives. While the public may view them as one monolithic group, there are actually two types of paparazzi: those invited to Hollywood events to take photos *and* those who scour the streets looking for unsuspecting celebrities. Those who are invited to the red carpet events are treated as press and expected to follow celebrities during the course of the event. Those images are a part of the publicity campaign for the spectacle. Once the red carpet event is finished, many celebrities expect the paparazzi to magically disappear and stay away until the next invited event. These same photographers may also work as freelance-for-hire paparazzi by standing outside a Beverly Hills or Hollywood restaurant waiting to capture someone's image.

There is a line between mainstream entertainment news photographers and paparazzi activities. Entertainment news is an accepted form of journalism, whereas paparazzi photos sold to various celebrity-focused magazines and websites such as *TMZ*, *People*, and *US Weekly* are often frowned upon by many celebrities. Yet, *L.A. Times* entertainment reporter Christina D'Zurilla explained that the line between the two is still shrinking, and her own work as an entertainment reporter is proof:

> I can't roll my eyes because up until the past year to year and a half I have been in a position where I feed off the paparazzi because I am doing celebrity coverage, but I am one of two people on our staff where we are following all the trending stories so no two people can cover the hundreds of trending stories there are by going out getting them ourselves.[66]

D'Zurilla often uses online paparazzi-sourced photos and headlines to start working on her own stories. As a reporter with the *L.A. Times*, she must responsibly verify all sources and reference the paparazzi materials as needed.

Regardless if it is a staged red carpet event or the unchoreographed photo, former *People* reporter and editor Belinda Cohen noted that many celebrity magazine and online publications buy a lot of their photos that are sourced from paparazzi.[67] Magazines such as *People*, *In Touch*, and *US Weekly* buy these non-exclusive photos. Exclusive photos which only one paparazzo shot and sold to one media outlet are bid on by different magazines and websites. Whichever publication is willing to pay the most, buys the photos. These magazines do not have staff photographers but instead rely on paparazzi for these visual materials of celebrities who are in Hollywood shopping, eating, and exercising. Cohen noted that most magazines stay away from the paparazzo photo surreptitiously taken on private property.[68] They do not want to be accused of violating privacy.

Regarding ethics, in recent years the celebrity and entertainment magazines have respected individual requests to respect family privacy, especially children. That includes Kristen Bell's Twitter #no children campaign discussed in chapter 1. Cohen noted many magazines look to the social media activity by celebrities themselves and then craft their own ethics publishing guidelines based on social media usage:

> Halle Berry never posts pictures of her children on social media. So, we respect that. So, if she is being photographed on the street with her child, we are not going to run those pictures versus a Kim Kardashian who will post pictures of children on social media, that's fair game.[69]

The proactive action by celebrities to share family photos on social media is fair game for the celebrity magazines. These basic ethical guidelines by celebrity magazines, as little as they are, are often more than those held by the paparazzi themselves.

Despite the plethora of professional journalism ethics guidelines that exist, very few, if any, paparazzi refer to them. Any ethics they incorporate are their own based on their personal beliefs. One of the indirect consequences of a lack of industry-wide paparazzi ethical guidelines was California's 2014 update to its privacy and anti-harassment laws to protect the public from overreaching paparazzi. Chapter 3 reviews and analyzes these laws in detail.

NOTES

1. Clémont Chéroux, Camille Lenglois, Véra Léon, and Max Bonhomme, "Hazards of the Trade: Interviews with Paparazzi," in *Paparazzi! Photographers, Stars, Artists* ed. Clément Chéroux (Paris: Flammarion, 2014), 37.
2. Ibid.
3. Ibid, 38.
4. Amy Gajda, *The First Amendment Bubble: How Privacy and Paparazzi Threaten a Free Press* (Cambridge, Massachusetts: Harvard University Press 2015), 151.
5. Ibid.
6. Ibid.
7. Ibid, 123.
8. Graeme Turner, "Is celebrity news, news?," *Journalism*, 15(2) (2014): 145.
9. Ibid.
10. Ibid.
11. Ibid.
12. Ibid, 146.
13. Ibid.
14. Ibid.
15. Kevin Frazier (co-host, *Entertainment Tonight*) in discussion with author, February 2018.
16. Ibid.
17. Vince Flores (photographer) in discussion with author, July 2019.

18. Christie D'Zurillo (entertainment reporter, *Los Angeles Times*) in discussion with author, February 2018.
19. Ibid.
20. Kevin Frazier (co-host, *Entertainment Tonight*) in discussion with author, February 2018.
21. Ibid.
22. Sam Kelogg [psued] (Getty, 20th Century FOX, and Instar Images freelance photographer) in discussion with author, February 2018.
23. Anne Jerslev and Mette Mortensen, "Taking the extra out of the extraordinary: Paparazzi photography as celebrity news genre on the Internet," *International Journal of Cultural Studies*, 17(6): 625.
24. Ibid.
25. Ibid., 624–25.
26. Ibid., 630.
27. Carol Squiers, "Class Struggle: The Invention of Paparazzi Photography and the Death of Diana, Princess of Wales," *Overexposed: Essays on Contemporary Photography* ed. Carol Squiers (New York, NY: The New Press, 1999), 271.
28. Clémont Chéroux, Camille Lenglois, Véra Léon, and Max Bonhomme, "Hazards of the Trade: Interviews with Paparazzi," in *Paparazzi! Photographers, Stars, Artists* ed. Clément Chéroux (Paris: Flammarion, 2014), 37.
29. Carol Squiers, Class Struggle: The Invention of Paparazzi Photography and the Death of Diana, Princess of Wales, *Overexposed: Essays on Contemporary Photography* ed. Carol Squiers (New York, NY: The New Press, 1999), 271.
30. Salma, Haidrani, "Charitable Celebrities: The Stars Who Give Back," *Glamour*, October 4, 2017, http://www.glamourmagazine.co.uk/gallery/charitable-celebrities-stars-who-do-good.
31. Carol Squiers, Class Struggle: The Invention of Paparazzi Photography and the Death of Diana, Princess of Wales, *Overexposed: Essays on Contemporary Photography* ed. Carol Squiers (New York, NY: The New Press, 1999), 271.
32. Ibid.
33. Ibid.
34. Ibid.
35. Cal. Civ. Code §1708.8 (2018).
36. David Burnett, (freelance photojournalist) in discussion with author, January 2018.
37. Ibid.
38. Christie D'Zurillo (entertainment reporter, *Los Angeles Times*) in discussion with author, February 2018.
39. Ibid.
40. David Burnett, (freelance photojournalist) in discussion with author, January 2018
41. Christie D'Zurillo (entertainment reporter, *Los Angeles Times*) in discussion with author, February 2018.
42. Ibid.
43. Ibid.
44. Frank LoMonte (Director, Brechner Center for Freedom of Information) in discussion with author, January 2018.
45. Ibid.
46. Society of Professional Journalists, Code of Ethics, accessed on February 27, 2018, http://www.spj.org/ethicscode.asp.
47. Ibid.
48. Ibid.
49. Radio Television Digital News Association Code of Ethics, accessed on February 27, 2018, https://www.rtdna.org/content/rtdna_code_of_ethics.
50. Ibid.
51. Ibid.

52. National Press Photographer's Association, Code of Ethics, accessed on February 27, 2018, https://nppa.org/code-ethics.
53. Ibid.
54. Clémont Chéroux, Camille Lenglois, Véra Léon, and Max Bonhomme, "Hazards of the Trade: Interviews with Paparazzi," in *Paparazzi! Photographers, Stars, Artists* ed. Clément Chéroux (Paris: Flammarion, 2014), 36.
55. Ibid.
56. Ibid.
57. Ibid.
58. Sam Kelogg [psued] (Getty, 20th Century FOX, and Instar Images freelance photographer) in discussion with author, February 2018.
59. Ibid.
60. Ibid.
61. Ibid.
62. Dale Jacquet, *Journalistic Ethics: Moral Responsibility in the Media* (Upper Saddle River, New Jersey: Pearson 2007), 205.
63. Ibid.
64. Ibid.
65. Ibid.
66. Christie D'Zurillo (entertainment reporter, *Los Angeles Times*) in discussion with author, February 2018.
67. Belinda Cohen [psued] (former *People* magazine editor and reporter) in discussion with author, March 2018.
68. Ibid.
69. Ibid.

THREE

California Laws Protecting Celebrities' Privacy

In the 1960s and 1970s, self-claimed "paparazzo" photographer Ron Gallela used a simple film camera to build a successful career based on his frequent photos of Jacqueline Kennedy Onassis and her family while they lived in New York City. He would physically place himself in front of the former First Lady and her children to capture their images. Onassis and the Secret Service sued him for invasion of privacy. In two separate court cases, Gallela unsuccessfully argued a legal right, based on the First Amendment freedom of the press, to photograph Onassis at his discretion.[1] A federal appellate court judge granted Onassis a physical zone of privacy of one hundred yards outside her New York City home and fifty yards outdoors away from her children.[2] The court order protected Onassis from "any blocking of her movement in public places and thoroughfares" or "taking any action which could reasonably be foreseen to harass, alarm, or frighten the children," and her children were guaranteed a right to enter their "schools or play areas."[3] This was a legal victory for Onassis decades before the often-intrusive paparazzi behavior we are now accustomed to.

Several decades later, according to law professor Amy Gajda, we now live in a "push-the-envelope media" world where technology is used as a tool to reveal private facts and publish them online.[4] A community of courts, attorneys, and lawmakers have been advocating for more privacy protections for years. There is an ongoing debate about the delicate balance between the need for privacy (including for public figures) and the constitutional right for the media to disseminate information to the public. Gallela, as a New York City–based paparazzo, was once at the center of this critical debate. Now L.A. paparazzi sit at the cornerstone of the privacy versus media rights issue.

Historically, the origins of modern-day privacy law date back to 1890, when Samuel Warren and Louis Brandeis published an article in the *Harvard Law Review* urging a right to privacy.[5] As with today's paparazzi, Warren and Brandeis pointedly criticized the media of their era for encroaching on individuals' privacy rights: "Instantaneous photographs and newspaper enterprise have invaded the sacred precincts of private and domestic life; and numerous mechanical devices threaten to make good the prediction that what is whispered in the closet shall be proclaimed from the house-tops."[6]

Both Warren and Brandeis were shocked by the intrusive press of their time in the late nineteenth century. Their 130 year-old concerns parallel today's often-heard criticism against the paparazzi:

> The press is overstepping in every direction the obvious bounds of propriety and of decency. Gossip is no longer the resource of the idle and of the vicious, but has become a trade, which is pursued with industry as well as effrontery. To satisfy a prurient taste the details of sexual relations are spread broadcast in the columns of the daily papers. To occupy the indolent, column upon column is filled with idle gossip, which can only be procured by intrusion upon the domestic circle.[7]

The newspaper gossip columns of the Warren and Brandeis era are our modern-day celebrity-focused television shows, websites, and social media posts. A simple website search using the phrase "paparazzi photos" or "celebrity photos" yields an unlimited number of stories and pictures from websites such as TMZ.com, Celebuzz.com, and eonline.com. According to Gajda, Warren and Brandeis's article had six themes that can be applied to paparazzi today: strong criticism of media, worries about technology use, our self-interest in defining privacy, balancing privacy against legitimate news stories, privacy interests for public figures, and privacy's overall role in society.[8]

Warren and Brandeis were alarmed that the press of their era overstepped bounds of "propriety and decency."[9] Gossip and discussions of sexual lives were becoming more apparent in the press.[10] They accurately pointed out that the supply for these stories filled the public's demand. Warren and Brandeis's commentary on using technology to foment unwarranted gossip-strewn stories focused on how cameras of their era were using film that could be developed within hours and then published in a newspaper the following day.[11]

The two legal scholars strongly advocated that it was up to individuals to decide if their own private information should be made public. The person's consent was vital.[12] When it came to the issue of what information the public had a legitimate right to know, Warren and Brandeis explained that materials concerning their professional, public activity were legitimate news. They argued that the only time the public needed to know about a private issue was when there was a direct connection to a person's public career.[13]

Any discussion of our modern-day privacy law needs to begin with a brief explanation of the four legal areas of privacy law that are often recognized at the state level. In 1960 William Prosser, who is considered one of the foremost experts in privacy, outlined the four areas of the modern-day invasion of privacy law: intrusion on an individual's physical solitude or seclusion; appropriation of one's name or likeness for financial benefit or harm; public disclosure of private facts; and placing someone in false light before the public.[14] Across the United States, each of these areas often stands alone as separate state laws.

Celebrities often accuse paparazzi of two out of the four privacy invasions: intrusion and private facts. According to Trager, Ross, and Reynolds, intrusion is the physical trespassing into people's lives.[15] In the twenty-first century, intrusive newsgathering techniques may include high-powered camera lenses, hidden microphones, or even using drones or infrared technology to track people. Intrusion may be physical, conducted in-person by a member of the media from technology.[16] The intruder violates the victim's solitude.

The second tort is public disclosure of private facts, the media obtaining true but confidential information that is of no public concern.[17] This might include the victim's finances, health information, intimate details of their life, or even facts related to their home life.[18] Any personal information that can be obtained from a public record is not considered a private fact. Private facts are those pieces of information anyone—private citizen or public figure—expect to remain undisclosed and kept confidential.

The next two areas of privacy are not directly related to the controversial actions of paparazzi but pertain to every American: appropriation and false light. Appropriation is using someone's name, photo, or voice without their permission for commercial, profit-making purposes.[19] False light, as its name indicates, is publishing or stating something about an individual that is simply not true and characterizes them in a false way. Unlike libel that harms the victim's reputation, false light may not actually harm someone's reputation depending on the circumstances.[20] Some states' laws link false light to libel and require victims to prove harm to reputation.

CALIFORNIA TAKES UP THE CELEBRITIES' CAUSE

Starting in 1998, the California legislature took an active approach in limiting the power of paparazzi to invade peoples' lives.[21] The term *paparazzi* is never actually written in the law, yet it's clear that they are the intended target. Recent updates to these laws focused on banning the use of drones and other advanced photo and video technology in order to safeguard privacy. Since their inception in 1998, the anti-paparazzi laws were strengthened in 2005, 2009, 2010, and then in 2014. The laws also impose fines, but not just on the paparazzi who take and sell photos. The media outlets who buy the images could also be fined if a judge rules those images invaded someone's privacy.

As discussed in detail later in this chapter, California has taken a proactive approach to protecting celebrities from intrusive paparazzi. Over the years, celebrities living in California appeared before the state assembly asking elected officials to pass laws protecting their personal and family privacy from physical intrusion on their lives. In 2013, Jennifer Garner and Halle Berry were instrumental in convincing the legislature to take action in tightening state privacy laws.[22] Both testified that paparazzi should not be allowed to follow their children. Berry stated her daughter feared going to school due to the daily presence of paparazzi.[23] The California State Legislature listened to Berry and Garner and passed SB 606, an amendment to the state's harassment laws. SB 606 criminalized "any person who intentionally harasses the child or ward of any other person because of that person's employment."[24] Essentially, it is a crime in California to harass any child or for the paparazzi to follow the children of celebrities based on the parent's profession. Prince Harry and Duchess Meghan Markle have issued legal complaints against paparazzi flying drones over their Santa Barbara, California home attempting to obtain photos of their son, Archie.

California, with its culture of celebrity and corporate home to television, film, and music industries, is not alone in protecting celebrities' private lives. Hawaii is a common vacation destination for California celebrities. In 2013 musician Steven Tyler actively but unsuccessfully lobbied state politicians to pass a privacy reform law. The Hawaiian state senate passed a privacy reform bill in 2013, but the state House of Representatives never brought it up for a vote.[25]

Despite Tyler's failure, Hawaii has a detailed invasion of privacy law that focuses on intrusion that is similar to California's law. Hawaiian law criminalizes any attempt to use a device to record images or sounds without the consent of the intended subject.[26] It is also a crime to obtain a nude or sexual image of a subject with the "intent to harm substantially the depicted person with respect to that person's health, safety, *business*, calling, *career, financial condition, reputation*, or personal relationships."[27] The italicized terms, *business, career, financial condition*, and *reputation* can all apply to celebrities vacationing at a Hawaiian beach or resort. Similar to California, the state's privacy law also includes banning the use of technology in an outdoor public location aimed at a private location "which would not ordinarily be audible or comprehensible outside."[28] Unlike California law, Hawaii does not impose direct financial penalties on media outlets that may purchase a photo or video from a freelance paparazzo.

New York City is another well-known celebrity hub. Surprisingly, New York state law does *not* recognize the invasion of privacy tort of intrusion. The *only* invasion of privacy law recognized under New York law is appropriation. This is surprising given New York's extensive entertainment and theater industries. New York privacy law focuses on any media organization that obtains a video or photograph of a subject (including celebrities) for commercial, for-profit reasons without their permission.[29] In a nod to the state's entertainment industry, it is a crime for anyone to sell someone's likeness without their permission.[30]

FIXING CALIFORNIA'S PAPARAZZI "PROBLEM" STARTING IN 1998

California is the national leader in passing legislation that protects all its residents from the paparazzi. California's anti-paparazzi laws, specifically Civil Code Sections 1708.7 and 1708.8, focus on two privacy torts: intrusion and disclosure of private facts. Most legal scholars wrote about paparazzi and the apparent need for California laws to protect privacy prior to the 2014 updates to the state law signed by Governor Jerry Brown. In 2010 constitutional law attorney Christina Locke analyzed the 1998 origins of California's anti-paparazzi laws.[31] Locke noted that an earlier version of Section 1708.8 focused on intrusion by preventing paparazzi from using enhanced cameras or video recorders to invade celebrities' privacy.[32]

In 2005, the California legislature updated 1708.8 again to include fines for any photos sold showing paparazzi assaulting celebrities.[33] This update included a provision for punishing media outlets with fines if they published these photos.[34] As Locke correctly observed, this runs afoul of the Supreme Court's decision in *Bartnicki v. Vopper*,[35] which found the First Amendment protects the media when it publishes information even if it was obtained in an illegal way.[36] She noted that in *Bartnicki*, the Court relied on *Florida Star v. BJF*[37] and *Smith v. Daily Mail*,[38] two earlier cases where it had ruled the media had the First Amendment right to republish information obtained legally even if that information invaded someone's privacy.[39]

Attorneys have attempted to provide practical solutions about celebrity complaints regarding paparazzi activities in Los Angeles. The idea of a "paparazzi-free zone" in California was proposed by entertainment attorney Tara Sattler in 2010.[40] She argued it would be a content neutral approach to protecting celebrities from the physical intrusion often associated with a hoard of paparazzi. Similar to the physical protection Jackie Onassis received from the courts in 1973, California law could guarantee a physical space of movement for everyone. There would be a clear space between anyone and paparazzi, a "personal safety zone."[41] The state legislature could determine the distance within a zone of privacy.

Sattler argued this buffer zone would not violate the First Amendment.[42] It would be both content neutral and narrowly tailored to meet a specific public need (physical safety for all Californians), and not more restrictive than necessary.[43] She noted that the Colorado Supreme Court upheld a similar law in 1999[44] and the U.S. Supreme Court upheld one even earlier in 1997,[45] and both decisions recognized the government's interest in providing a physical safety zone in the name of public safety. The U.S and Colorado Supreme Court decisions provided legal precedent for the California legislature if it chooses to one day move forward with a physical zone of privacy law.

In 2011 Attorney Cameron Danly suggested a two-part test to protect celebrity privacy without infringing on press rights.[46] Part one of the test is whether there is any overt interference with a person's physical ability to conduct their casual, day-to-day lives.[47] The second part of the test determines if their independent movements are a matter of public interest.[48] Danly noted that an invasion of privacy would occur if there is physical interference with someone's ability to conduct their daily activities, and if knowledge about the celebrity's movements are not in the public interest. Thus, if a celebrity must use a back door of a restaurant; employ decoy vehicles to confuse the paparazzi; or wear a wig to move about in public, then there is interference with that person's independence.[49] Such interference would only be acceptable if there is a public interest matter at hand. Danly acknowledged that defining the "public interest" is not easy but observed that a photo of a celebrity buying coffee at Starbucks may not qualify as public interest.[50]

In 2015 Matthew Lee wrote that California's best approach to safeguarding celebrities' privacy is to focus on their children.[51] By focusing on children's right to privacy, the state legislature can avoid any thorny constitutional issues regarding the First Amendment right to freedom of the press. A law focused on protecting minors can be narrowly tailored with specific restrictions. Media outlets could be fined if they publish photographs or video images of celebrity's children.[52] As minors, these children have a fundamental right to privacy that their famous adult parents do not have. Lee advocates that a hefty fine would discourage paparazzi and the agencies they sell photos to from invading the minors' privacy.[53]

Professor Emily Rehm (2017) advocated that the best legal approach to ensuring the constitutionality of anti-paparazzi statutes are to craft them based on the 1968 *O'Brien* test.[54] The Supreme Court in *U.S. v. O'Brien* provided a three-part test for regulating speech activities without running afoul of the First Amendment.[55] Government regulation is justified if (1) it furthers an important or substantial governmental interest; (2) that governmental interest is unrelated to the content of the speech;

and (3) restrictions on that speech are no more than what is necessary to accomplish the government interest.[56] Rhem argued that anti-paparazzi statutes would be constitutional under the O'Brien test since they focus on the public's safety (including celebrities and their families), an important government interest.[57] Under the O'Brien test scenario, paparazzi photographers can conduct their work as long as the public (celebrities) are not placed in any harm's way.

PAPARAZZI ENDANGERING MOTORISTS

California passed a law in 2011 that reflects the O'Brien approach to speech regulation. Section 40008 of the California Vehicle Code criminalizes driving recklessly while capturing photos or videos of an individual in another vehicle.[58] In the 2015 case, *Raef v. Appellate Division of the Superior County of Los Angeles,* a California appeals court reviewed the arrest of paparazzo photographer Paul Raef, who was charged with violating Section 40008 of the California Vehicle Code.[59] Raef was cited for driving recklessly to capture images of celebrity Justin Beiber, who was also speeding on a California highway. Authorities arrested Raef for willfully driving in disregard for the safety of other motorists with the intent of capturing a photo of Bieber for a "commercial purpose."

Section 40008 is part of the California vehicle code which is similar to Sections 1708.8 and 1708.7 of the state's civil code in that it targets potential physical actions by anyone, including the paparazzi.[60] The statute focuses on conduct of a photographer beyond the intent to take photos or videos.[61] As Matthew Lee noted in 2015, the law aims at how photographers *obtain* content, not the actual photo or video materials, an *O'Brien* legal approach to the law.[62] The law criminalizes any reckless driving with the intent of capturing an image for a commercial purpose.[63] It may be a "visual image, sound recording, or other physical impression of another person."[64] Anyone found guilty is imprisoned for up to six months *and* fined up to $2,500.[65] So far, the *Raef* decision is the *only* legal court test to any of California's anti-paparazzi laws. In *Raef* the California appeals court ruled that Section 40008 of California's Vehicle Code was constitutional and not an infringement of his First Amendment rights.[66]

Raef argued that Section 40008 abridged his First Amendment rights as a member of the media, arguing that the law was a content-based restriction. In 2012, the trial court ruled for Raef, but the Appellate Division of the Los Angeles County Superior Court reversed in 2013 and convicted him.[67] The Court of Appeal for California's Second Appellate District agreed with the superior court and upheld the decision. The court's three judges reiterated that Section 40008 is not an infringement of press rights. It is a time, place, and manner law (O'Brien test) that focuses on the safety of California drivers and therefore not a content-based speech or press restriction.[68] In the decision, Judge Norman Epstein wrote the law is not aimed specifically at any media, including the paparazzi:

> On its face, section 40008 is not limited to paparazzi chasing celebrities or reporters gathering news. Instead, the statute targets 'any person' who commits an enumerated traffic offense with the intent to capture the image, sound, or physical impression of 'another person' for a commercial purpose.[69]

Epstein noted that the law's intent was not aimed at newsgathering activities.[70] The vehicle code ordinance applies to anyone (media or otherwise) who attempts to disrupt traffic to obtain images for commercial use.[71] Raef further argued that Section 40008 hampers speech rights by including members of the media who may speed on the roads to cover a breaking news story. The court disagreed. Judge Epstein stated that the law is narrowly tailored to keep drivers safe from anyone who may try to obtain photos while driving recklessly.[72] It is the physical act of taking photos or video while driving that is a safety concern, not the idea of gathering images.[73]

The *Raef* decision provides some legal guidance concerning the constitutionality of Sections 1708.8 and 1708.7 of California's Civil Code. These invasion of privacy and anti-stalking laws aimed at protecting the physical welfare of victims may withstand further First Amendment scrutiny by California state courts. If drivers' safety is what drove the appeals court to uphold the constitutionality of the vehicle statute, then that same jurisprudence may lend legal credence to California's privacy-based intrusion and stalking laws discussed below.

APPLYING PRIVACY INTRUSION LAW TO PAPARAZZI PHOTOGRAPHY

On September 30, 2014, Governor Jerry Brown signed into law two bills aimed at the paparazzi. One of the laws, California Assembly Bill No. 2306, Section 1708.8 of the Civil Code, is aimed at the heart of paparazzi activities. It encompasses issues related to invasion of privacy stemming from the intrusion tort.[74] The law uses the intrusion privacy tort to criminalize capturing a person's (including family) image either in-person or with advanced photo technology. It also extends the tort of intrusion to punish paparazzi and the media outlets who buy their photos.[75]

The law has two overall components: physical and constructive invasion of privacy. The physical invasion of privacy occurs when the "defendant commits a physical trespass in attempting to capture the image or recording."[76] The constructive invasion is using technology when the physical intrusion is not possible: "the defendant captures the image or recording, without a physical trespass, through the use of a 'visual or auditory enhancing' device to capture an image or recording that could only have been obtained by a physical trespass in the absence of the device."[77] Telephoto lenses and shotgun microphones are examples of "enhancing" devices.

An intrusion crime occurs when victims (celebrities) are located on their property and engaged in "personal or familial activity."[78] The law prohibits anyone—ostensibly paparazzi—from using "any device" including drones to capture images above private property. It is illegal to violate one's privacy "through the use of any device, regardless of whether there is a physical trespass."[79] The law is similar to Hawaii's privacy law since it focuses on using technology in ostensibly public areas to capture images of private personal activities. Prince Harry and Meghan Markle's complaints about the paparazzi flying drones over their Santa Barbara home are based on this part of the law.

While the goal of protecting family privacy is laudable, this provision of California law is, nonetheless, problematic. A future legal challenge in state or federal could be focused on the law's prohibition of drones. The California Assembly's Floor Analysis, prior to passage of the law, referred to the potential use of a drone as a means of invading a subject's privacy: "a drone with a standard (as opposed to "enhanced") camera or microphone could achieve the same (or even more detailed) images than could an enhanced device used from afar."[80] Arguably, California should not have legislated restrictions on drone usage even to protect someone's privacy; rather that is the jurisdiction of the Federal Aviation Authority.[81] FAA rules on drones state that media organizations must have permission to fly a drone by applying for a waiver to operate it.[82] Media are considered commercial operators and need to obtain a specialized, commercial operators permit to operate a drone.[83] The media must demonstrate to the FAA that its proposed use of a drone will not harm public safety.[84]

Any photographer who operates a drone for commercial purposes on behalf of a media organization must register the vehicle.[85] Even private, commercial, or hobby use of a drone must be registered with the FAA.[86] As with any federal government agency, the rules for operating a drone are often amended. State authorities and private companies can operate drones, but permission still originates from the FAA. No state government, including California, can mandate any rules about use of a drone. Even more importantly, at any time the FAA may impose new or altered regulations on commercial drone use.

The overall goal of section 1708.8 is to protect family privacy. Yet the law's definition of personal or familial activity is vague and overbroad, another weakness in the law. It defines personal or family activity as any intimate details of a subject's personal life; interactions among the subject's family where there is a "reasonable expectation of privacy"; activities on the subject's property; and "other aspects" of the subject's private affairs.[87] Personal activities and other aspects are not defined. Are *all* activities on personal property included in the law? Does this include activities that could be considered public and/or newsworthy such as a political event at someone's home or an outdoor neighborhood crime watch activity? What does "other aspects" of a subject's private affairs mean? Is it an activity? These questions show that these provisions of the law based on the privacy intrusion tort may not withstand First Amendment scrutiny because they are vague. If the goal of the California State Assembly is to protect celebrities' privacy rights, it is important for the legislature or the state courts to further delineate family privacy rights on personal property.

PUNISHING MEDIA FOR PUBLISHING OR BROADCASTING CONTENT

California law connects the sale of images for a "commercial purpose" to Section 1708.8's punishment for invasion of privacy.[88] The fine is between $5,000 and $50,000.[89] The commercial purpose provision of the law is problematic with respect to the First Amendment's freedom of press clause. It is defined as "any act done with the expectation of a sale, financial gain, or other consideration.[90] A commercial purpose can also relate to anyone who "directs, solicits, actually induces, or actually causes another person" to violate the law.[91] Essentially, if a member of the paparazzi works full-time for a media firm or is hired on a freelance basis, that company becomes financially liable for the actions performed by its contracted employees.

The financial relationships between paparazzi and media agencies is covered in the law. The commercial purpose section of 1708.8 (1)(e) could be interpreted as a content-based restriction, where any court would apply the legal strict scrutiny test to determine if the law violates the First Amendment. The U.S. Supreme Court defines a content-based law as one where the government (local, state, or federal) censors material it views unfavorably.[92] To pass strict scrutiny, a law must use the least restrictive means possible to censor the speech and advance a compelling government interest.[93] "Least restrictive" means that any law censors a minimal amount of content or activity for a very specific purpose. Typically, that purpose is related to the physical safety of society—that is, public health—a defendant's right to a fair trial, or national security.

On the surface, 1708.8's imposition of fines on the media might not pass the strict scrutiny test as a least restrictive approach to dissuade the media from publishing. Section 1708.8(2) requires the plaintiff (celebrity) to prove the media *knowingly* or *directly* told an employee to break the law. This plaintiff has to provide actual proof, a high and perhaps unreasonable burden.[94] The law's imposition of fines on paparazzi and media companies is a content-based restriction. Media firms would be fined for publishing material that they have a constitutional right to receive. Fair or not, previous U.S. Supreme Court decisions protect the media who publish or transmit any material that is initially collected illegally under certain circumstances and without the media's knowledge.[95]

National Press Photographer Association and First Amendment attorney Mickey Osterreicher concurs that 1708.8 is an informal move toward self-censorship by the press: "It creates that chilling effect of having a civil penalty hanging over your head."[96] He worries that under the law, paparazzi photography—as a profession—will be considered non-journalistic, and therefore subject to unconstitutional constraints. The result is the state categorizing paparazzi photographers as different from other photojournalists: "People can too easily write off photographers as paparazzi and think all of a sudden that they're subject to different requirements than any other journalist who has been assigned to photograph someone."[97]

Content-based restrictions often include any formal or informal forms of prior restraint. This means that the government is censoring what can be published. By imposing fines on the media for publishing images or audio, the law chills free speech and press coverage. While not an outright or overt form of prior restraint, the California legislature is endorsing, through fines, what kind of content it believes the public has the right to receive, a form of government empowerment over the media.[98] One of the hallmarks of First Amendment jurisprudence is government not favoring a form or category of speech in the marketplace of ideas. California may be punishing one idea in favor of another, mainstream, less controversial means of taking and publishing photos. A paparazzo photographer or media company that buys these photographs are at a disadvantage under the law. If there is going to be a constitutional challenge to Section 1708.8, it may well be focused on these financial penalties. As noted, historically, the Supreme Court is skeptical of any law that imposes a fine based on speech activity. Any decision that strikes down this part of the law would be in line with the Court's other rulings discussed in this chapter.

USING ANTI-HARASSMENT LAWS TO LIMIT PAPARAZZI ACTIVITIES

On the same day that Governor Brown signed into law Section 1708.8, he also added his signature to an update to the state's anti-harassment statute, Assembly Bill No. 1356, Section 1708.7 of the Civil Code.[99] The law protects victims from harassment, but its verbiage could be interpreted in a manner that would restrict paparazzi and violate their First Amendment rights. Based on California's existing stalking law, 1708.7 focuses on any perpetrator who places a victim under near constant surveillance, as paparazzi often do.[100] Victims must provide evidence they were followed, harassed, or placed under surveillance.[101] Additionally, victims must prove they feared for their personal or their family's safety and, as a result, suffered emotional distress.[102]

The defendant must make a "credible threat"—either verbally or physically.[103] A credible threat is defined as verbal or written patterns of conduct via:

> any action, method, device, or means, *follows, harasses, monitors, surveils,* threatens, or interferes with or damages the plaintiff's property, or a combination of verbal, written, or electronically communicated statements and conduct, made with the intent and apparent ability to carry out the threat so as to cause the person who is the target of the threat to reasonably fear for his or her safety or the safety of his or her immediate family.[104]

Paparazzi often *follow, monitor,* and *surveil* celebrities. Victims may view these actions as harassment. The counterargument is that what the victim views as harassment is simply the paparazzi's reporting on their subjects, even from a distance. Attorney Mickey Osterreicher points out that harassment is a subjective term: "What is an annoyance to one person could be welcoming to another. 'Oh you want to take my picture? That's great.' Again, these overly broad and vague terms are problematic."[105]

Whether we like it or not, paparazzi follow celebrities to film them or take their picture. In the course of their job, the photographers are following and monitoring their subjects. These are protected actions under the law as long as there is no threat of physical harm on the intended subject.[106] Stalking under state law includes a "pattern of conduct" which is defined as a series of acts that have a purpose to them.[107] This portion of the law is also problematic. The inherent nature of a paparazzo's job is a systemic pattern of conduct by monitoring celebrities including the day-to-day tracking of their activities in public places. Are California authorities going to arrest paparazzi on stalking charges when watching celebrities is the norm of the profession? This part of the statute violates the media's abilities to conduct its job in a protected manner according to the First Amendment.

Another aspect of Section 1708.7 prohibits stalking someone by using electronic communications, including cell phones and video cameras.[108] It may run into First Amendment challenges by celebrity-focused media operations such as TMZ.com. They could argue they have a right to keep tabs on celebrities whose lives are in the public eye. TMZ.com founder Harvey Levin has stated he believes the constant monitoring of celebrities is a newsworthy activity.[109]

The "Harvey Levins" of the world may also find another provision of the law problematic. Section 1708.7 defines what it means to follow a subject. The law states it means to move "in relative proximity" to the victim and exempts any "newsgathering conduct connected to a newsworthy event."[110] In the 1960s and 1970s, Ron Galella moved within "proximity" to Jackie Onassis and her family even after the court-ordered restrictions against him.[111] Not all paparazzi stake out celebrity homes. Many go to public venues such as the Los Angeles International Airport or they stand on sidewalks in front of trendy restaurants and night clubs. These locations are in relative proximity to celebrities. The media have a constitutional right to be physically located near their subjects.

As a whole, Section 1708.7 provides an exemption for "newsgathering conduct."[112] Yet, nowhere in the statute is the term defined. Paparazzi, as well as celebrity-based publications, television shows, and websites contend they are news-based. *E! News*, which is the website platform for E! Entertainment Television and owned by NBC Universal, considers itself a celebrity news operation: "We eat, sleep and breathe pop culture, delivering exclusive breaking news and in-depth coverage on celebrities, awards show and movie premiere livestreams, TV scoops and spoilers, fashion trends and tips, and what's viral now."[113]

Another vague provision of Section 1708.7 is the term "harass." It means annoy along with "alarms, torments, or terrorizes the victim."[114] The victim must prove emotional distress.[115] Paparazzi certainly "annoy" their subjects at times. But how would a celebrity victim prove emotional distress from being annoyed? This portion of the law is vague. It does not provide definitions to the terms "annoy or alarm." This is another area in which the California State Assembly or courts need to take another look and provide clarity on how annoy can lead to harassment.

Section 1708.7 requires victims to prove they or their legal team communicated with the defendant to stop the different forms of harassment.[116] This makes sense for anyone threatening physical harm to a victim. Yet, in the case of paparazzi, they are often told by celebrities and their representatives to stop the "harassment." The fundamental legal issue may come down to whether paparazzi are considered reporters and therefore are reporting and producing newsworthy stories as defined by this statute. If a California court were to rule that celebrity activity is newsworthy, does that mean pushy paparazzi are not harassing their subjects?

Take together the provisions of Section 1708.7 that a federal court, including the Supreme Court, could hear arguments about are the vagueness of the term "newsgathering conduct," the implications of "harass" when applied to the media, and the mandated official communications by any celebrity toward a paparazzo to stop the harassment. All three of these areas are fraught with constitutional weaknesses when applied to media including paparazzi. The fundamental job of any media organization and its staff is to keep tabs on the individuals at the center of a story. This is especially relevant in Los Angeles, home to the nation's entertainment industry. As noted in this chapter, there is a lot of legal precedent to find these provisions of the law unconstitutional.

One *potential* source of clarification on whether paparazzi are considered media under California law may be the state's shield law. Shield laws protect reporters from divulging the identity of confidential sources before state grand juries. For that specific purpose, California's shield law defines a member of the media as: "a publisher, editor, reporter, or other person connected with or employed upon a newspaper, magazine, or other periodical publication, or by a press association or wire service."[117] While the law applies to media who protect confidential sources, nonetheless, it provides a legal definition of media in the state. A California appellate court even recognized the shield law as including online media who produce content.[118] If state courts recognize the works of TMZ.com and celebuzz.com as media, then Section 1708.7's anti-harassment measure simply may not apply to paparazzi.

Attorney Mickey Osterreicher has tried to convince state legislatures—including California's—to apply its shield law to the privacy laws to clear up who can be prosecuted for privacy violations: "There is a direct conflict with the state shield law but unfortunately there are too many legislators in California and Hawaii in particular who pander to this constituency of 'Okay there are stars and celebrities so we will give them whatever they ask for' and they don't really think much beyond that."[119] It is up to the state legislature and courts to decide if the definition of media in the shield law should apply to paparazzi. Clarification on this issue could also narrow the state's stalking law's provisions discussed in this section including the relevant newsworthy event exemptions. If California applies the shield law definition of media to this harassment law, then the status of paparazzi would be clarified.

OVERALL ASSESSMENT OF CALIFORNIA'S PRIVACY AND STALKING LAWS

TMZ.com's founder, Harvey Levin, says that he runs a legitimate news operation.[120] If that's the case, his reporters, who often act as paparazzi in how they pursue celebrity stories, could be prosecuted under parts of Sections 1708.8 and 1708.7 of California's Civil Code. He could argue that the laws are unconstitutional as written since they bar the professional activities of his reporters: record, monitor, and conduct surveillance on celebrities. TMZ hires staff to monitor celebrities' movements and pays informants who assist in gathering information.[121] If TMZ is considered a news operation, then even these informants may be the equivalent of paid freelance staff, and thus potentially exempt under portions of these two laws. Other media agencies who publish paparazzi-sourced photos such as Getty or Bauer-Griffin need the laws on their side too.

As the analysis in this chapter shows, the specific provisions of California laws 1708.8 and 1708.7 that focus only on the intrusion and stalking torts are legal because they are content neutral focusing on time, place, and manner regulations. The laws do not violate the First Amendment rights of the press. Section 40008 of California's Vehicle Code is also a time, place, and manner restriction on anyone who drives and takes photos, namely the paparazzi.[122]

The main legal hurdle for the privacy-based intrusion law is the provision that fines the media for publishing photos if there is an invasion of privacy allegation. It may not withstand First Amendment scrutiny. Imposing a fine on the media for publishing or broadcasting content initially obtained legally or illegally by a journalist or paparazzi has broad free press consequences. As discussed, the Supreme Court gives the press wide latitude to publish content. California is clearly playing favorites with this content-based restriction as a light form of prior restraint. It has not met the hurdles the Supreme Court has provided over the years for censoring publications and broadcasts.

Section 1708.8's ban on using a drone to photograph people on private property is certainly laudable. Yet, the state simply does not have authority in this area. The FAA is the legal federal authority to determine who may use a drone for professional purposes. The FAA respects California privacy law, but it monitors airspace drone usage and provides permission for media entities to operate a drone. The FAA states that it seeks to partner with state authorities on drafting laws that are compliant with federal aviation rules.[123]

The anti-stalking law, Section 1708.7, has serious First Amendment implications as well. *Following, monitoring, surveilling, and annoying* are four terms used to define harassment in the law. It simply does not clear constitutional hurdles. These are vague and broad terms that could apply to any member of the mainstream press or a freelance reporter and photographer as they do their jobs. It is urgent that either the State Assembly or state courts amend these problematic areas of both laws. Press rights, even for those whose jobs are controversial, are a bedrock of the constitutional free press guarantee.

NOTES

1. *Galella v. Onassis*, 487 F.2d 986 (2d Cir. 1973).
2. Ibid., 998. Onassis was given a twenty-five-foot protective zone from Gallela and her children were provided thirty feet.
3. Ibid.
4. Amy Gajda, *The First Amendment Bubble* (Cambridge, Massachusetts: Harvard University Press, 2015), 157.

5. Samuel D. Warren & Louis Brandeis, "The Right to Privacy," *Harvard Law Review* (1890): 193.
6. Ibid., 195.
7. Ibid., 195–96.
8. Amy Gajda, *The First Amendment Bubble* (Cambridge, Massachusetts: Harvard University Press, 2015), 159.
9. Warren and Brandeis, 196.
10. Ibid.
11. Ibid., 195.
12. Ibid., 199.
13. Ibid., 216.
14. William L. Prosser, "Privacy" *California Law Review* 48 (1960): 383.
15. Robert Trager, Susan Dente Ross, and Amy Reynolds, *The Law of Journalism and Mass Communication* (Los Angeles: Sage, 2016), 281.
16. Ibid.
17. Ibid., 286.
18. Ibid., 287.
19. Ibid., 266.
20. Ibid., 261.
21. Cal. Civ. Code §1708.8 (1998).
22. Reuters, "California bill protecting children of celebrities from paparazzi signed into law," *Daily News*, September 25, 2013, http://www.nydailynews.com/news/national/halle-berry-jennifer-garner-supported-california-bill-protecting-children-paparazzi-signed-law-article-1.1467192. Garner and Berry testified that paparazzi should not be allowed to follow their children who are out of the public eye.
23. Ibid.
24. Cal. Penal Code § 11414 (2014).
25. Lawrence Downes, "Looks Like the Steven Tyler Act' Is Sunk," *New York Times*, March 21, 2013. http://takingnote.blogs.nytimes.com/2013/03/21/looks-like-the-steven-tyler-act-is-sunk/.
26. HRS § 711-1110.9 (2016).
27. HRS § 711-1110.9 (2016).
28. HRS § 711-1111(1)(e) (2016).
29. NY CLS Civ R § 51 (2016).
30. Ibid.
31. Christina M. Locke, "Does Anti-Paparazzi Mean Anti-Press? First Amendment Implications of Privacy Legislation for the Newsroom," *Seton Hall Journal of Sports & Entertainment Law*, no. 20 (2010): 227.
32. Ibid., 237.
33. Ibid., 240.
34. Ibid.
35. 532 U.S. 514 (2001).
36. Locke, "Does Anti-Paparazzi Mean Anti-Press?," 241.
37. 491 U.S. 524 (1989). In *Florida Star v. BJF*, the Supreme Court upheld the right of the *Florida Star* newspaper to publish the identity of a sexual assault victim since it obtained her identity in a legal manner, from the newspaper's public file.
38. 443 U.S. 97 (1979). In *Smith v. Daily Mail Publishing Co.*, the Supreme Court ruled that the media could publish the identity of a minor involved in a shooting even though it obtained the name through investigative reporting of witnesses.
39. Locke, "Does Anti-Paparazzi Mean Anti-Press?," 242.
40. Tara Sattler, "Comment, Plagued by the Paparazzi: How California Should Sharpen the Focus on Its Not-So Picture Perfect Paparazzi Laws," *Southwest Law Review*, no. 40 (2010): 403.
41. Ibid., 415.
42. Ibid., 416. Sattler stated that proposed law would be constitutional for three reasons: "(1) the paparazzi-free zone law is a content neutral law; (2) the paparazzi-

free zone law is narrowly tailored to serve a significant government interest; and (3) the paparazzi-free zone law leaves open ample alternative means for communication."

43. Ibid.

44. See *Hill v. Thomas*, 973 P.2d 1246, 1255 (Colo. 1999).

45. See *Schenck v. Pro Choice Network*, 519 U.S. 357 (1997).

46. Cameron Danly, "Paparazzi and the Search for Federal Legislation," *Washington State University Law Review*, no. 38 (2011): 161.

47. Ibid., 170.

48. Ibid.

49. Ibid.

50. Ibid.

51. Matthew Lee, "Strict Liability and the Anti-Paparazzi Act: The Best Solution to Protect Children of Celebrities," *Hastings Law Journal Online*, no. 66 (2015): 24.

52. Ibid.

53. Ibid.

54. Emily Rehm, "Breaking News and Breaking the Law: Reining in California's Criminalization of Paparazzi and the Intent to Photograph," *Southwestern Law Review*, no. 46 (2017): 478.

55. 391 U.S. 367 (1968).

56. Ibid.

57. Rehm, "Breaking News and Breaking the Law," 478.

58. Cal. Veh. Code §40008 (2018).

59. 240 Cal. App. 4th 1112 (2015).

60. Cal. Veh. Code §40008 (a)(2018). "any person who violates Section 21701, 21703, or 23103, with the intent to capture any type of visual image, sound recording, or other physical impression of another person for a commercial purpose, is guilty of a misdemeanor and not an infraction and shall be punished by imprisonment in a county jail for not more than six months and by a fine of not more than two thousand five hundred dollars ($2,500)."

61. Rehm, "Breaking News and Breaking the Law," 481.

62. Matthew Lee, "Strict Liability and the Anti-Paparazzi Act: The Best Solution to Protect Children of Celebrities," 18.

63. Rehm, "Breaking News and Breaking the Law," 481.

64. Ibid.

65. Ibid.

66. 240 Cal. App. 4th 1112 (2015).

67. Ibid.

68. Ibid., 1125.

69. Ibid., 1121.

70. Ibid., 1122.

71. Ibid.

72. Ibid., 1138.

73. Ibid., 1140.

74. Cal. Civ. Code §1708.8 (2018).

75. Ibid.

76. Cal. Civ. Code §1708.8 (l)(1) (2018). According to this part of the law, any form of advanced technology from telephoto lenses to heat-based infrared sensors to drones may not be used to impede on someone's invasion of privacy on their property while engaged in "personal or familial activity."

77. Ibid.

78. Cal. Civ. Code §1708.8 (1)(a) (2018). The law states "A person is liable for physical invasion of privacy when the defendant knowingly enters onto the land of another person without permission or otherwise committed a trespass in order to physically invade the privacy of the plaintiff with the intent to capture any type of visual image, sound recording, or other physical impression of the plaintiff engaging in a personal

or familial activity and the physical invasion occurs in a manner that is offensive to a reasonable person."

79. Cal. Civ. Code §1708.8 (1) (b) (2018). While not specifically mentioning the use of drone, the law infers it, "A person is liable for constructive invasion of privacy when the defendant attempts to capture, in a manner that is offensive to a reasonable person, any type of visual image, sound recording, or other physical impression of the plaintiff engaging in a personal or familial activity under circumstances in which the plaintiff had a reasonable expectation of privacy, through the use of any device, regardless of whether there is a physical trespass, if this image, sound recording, or other physical impression could not have been achieved without a trespass unless the device was used.

80. AB 2306 CHAU Concurrence in Senate Amendments, 2014 Leg. Sess. (CA 2014).

81. The Federal Aviation Administration is the federal agency that has jurisdiction over air space used for commercial purposes, including the use of drones. The FAA, not state authorities, can regulate air space. Additionally, any media organization in California or any other state that may want to use a drone must contract with a company who has obtained the proper approvals or certification from the FAA or seek such approvals itself. See Sovereignty and Use of Airspace 49 U.S.C. §40103 (2015); Federal Aviation Administration, Unmanned Aircraft Systems (UAS) Frequently Asked Questions (2016) (available at https://www.faa.gov/uas/faq/#qn20).

82. Unmanned Aircraft Systems (UAS) Frequently Asked Questions/Help, Federal Aviation Administration, https://www.faa.gov/uas/faqs/#fwb.

83. Certified Remote Pilots Including Commercial Operators, Federal Aviation Administration, https://www.faa.gov/uas/commercial_operators/. A media organization may obtain a permit to fly a drone that is under the Small UAS rule (drone under 55 pounds).

84. Unmanned Aircraft Systems (UAS) Frequently Asked Questions/Help, Federal Aviation Administration, https://www.faa.gov/uas/faqs/#fwb.

85. Ibid.

86. Ibid.

87. Cal. Civ. Code §1708.8 (7)(i)(1)(2018). For the purposes of this section, "private, personal, and familial activity" includes, but is not limited to:

a. Intimate details of the plaintiff's personal life under circumstances in which the plaintiff has a reasonable expectation of privacy.
b. Interaction with the plaintiff's family or significant others under circumstances in which the plaintiff has a reasonable expectation of privacy.
c. If and only after the person has been convicted of violating Section 626.8 of the Penal Code, any activity that occurs when minors are present at any location set forth in subdivision (a) of Section 626.8 of the Penal Code.
d. Any activity that occurs on a residential property under circumstances in which the plaintiff has a reasonable expectation of privacy.
e. Other aspects of the plaintiff's private affairs or concerns under circumstances in which the plaintiff has a reasonable expectation of privacy.

88. Cal. Civ. Code §1708.8 (1) (d) (2018).

89. Ibid.

90. Cal. Civ. Code §1708.8 (7)(k) (2018).

91. Cal. Civ. Code §1708.8 (1)(e) (2018).

92. *U.S. v. Johnson*, 491 US 397 (1989) and *U.S. v. Eichman*, 496 US 310 (1990). In both cases, the Supreme Court ruled that state and federal laws prohibiting the desecration of the American flag were content based, an unconstitutional violation of the First Amendment free speech clause.

93. Robert Trager, Joseph Russomanno, Susan Dente Ross, and Amy Reynolds, *The Law of Journalism and Mass Communications* (Washington, D.C.: Sage/CQ Press 2016), 71.

94. Under Section 1708.8(2), any plaintiff would have to prove the media directed their employee to break the law or had "actual knowledge" that that the media firm directed a paparazzi employee to break broke the law to capture a photo or record video. Cal. Civ. Code §1708.8 (1)(f)(1) (2018). In order for the media company to be fined, the law requires that the plaintiff show proof of actual knowledge by proving "awareness, understanding, and recognition," obtained prior to the time the photo or video was sold to a media company. Ibid. §1708.8 (1)(f)(2) (2014). In addition to actual knowledge, the plaintiff would have to prove that the paparazzi were compensated for the materials that are published.

95. *Bartnicki v. Vopper*, 532 U.S. 514 (2001).

96. Mickey Osterreicher (attorney) in discussion with author, January 2018.

97. Ibid.

98. *Near v. Minnesota*, 283 U.S. 697 (1931). In this case, the U.S. Supreme Court outlined the components of government imposed prior restraint: government oversight of speech or publication; government chooses what speech or content is acceptable; and provides government with power to ban the content. The Court ruled that prior restraint is presumptively invalid except in an unusual circumstance such as war.

99. Cal. Civ. Code §1708.7 (2018).

100. California Legislative Counsel's Digest AB 1356 (2014).

101. Cal. Civ. Code §1708.7 (1) (2018).

102. Cal. Civ. Code §1708.7 (2) (A) – (B) (2018). "(A) The plaintiff reasonably feared for his or her safety, or the safety of an immediate family member. For purposes of this subparagraph, 'immediate family' means a spouse, parent, child, any person related by consanguinity or affinity within the second degree, or any person who regularly resides, or, within the six months preceding any portion of the pattern of conduct, regularly resided, in the plaintiff's household.(B) The plaintiff suffered substantial emotional distress, and the pattern of conduct would cause a reasonable person to suffer substantial emotional distress."

103. Cal. Civ. Code §1708.7 (3)(A) (2018). "The defendant, as a part of the pattern of conduct specified in paragraph (1), made a credible threat with either (i) the intent to place the plaintiff in reasonable fear for his or her safety, or the safety of an immediate family member, or (ii) reckless disregard for the safety of the plaintiff or that of an immediate family member. In addition, the plaintiff must have, on at least one occasion, clearly and definitively demanded that the defendant cease and abate his or her pattern of conduct and the defendant persisted in his or her pattern of conduct unless exigent circumstances make the plaintiff's communication of the demand impractical or unsafe."

104. Cal. Civ. Code §1708.7 (3)(B)(2)(2018). Author's italicization.

105. Mickey Osterreicher (attorney) in discussion with author, January 2018.

106. Cal. Civ. Code §1708.7 (3)(A)(2018).

107. Cal. Civ. Code §1708.7 (3)(B)(1) (2018).

108. Cal. Civ. Code §1708.7 (3)(B)(3)(2018). "Electronic communication device includes, but is not limited to, telephones, cellular telephones, computers, video recorders, fax machines, or pagers."

109. Nicholas Schmidle, "The Digital Dirt: How TMZ Gets the Videos and Photos that Celebrities Want to Hide," *The New Yorker*, February 22, 2013, http://www.newyorker.com/magazine/2016/02/22/inside-harvey-levins-tmz.

110. Cal. Civ. Code §1708.7 (3)(B)(4)(2017).

111. *Galella v. Onassis*, 487 F.2d 986 (2d Cir. 1973).

112. Cal. Civ. Code §1708.7 (3)(B)(b)(4) and Cal. Civ. Code §1708.7 (3)(B)(b)(6) (2018).

113. "Who We Are," About Us, *E! News*, last modified October 19, 2014, http://www.eonline.com/about.

114. Cal. Civ. Code §1708.7 (3)(B)(5)(2018). "Harass" means a knowing and willful course of conduct directed at a specific person which seriously alarms, annoys, torments, or terrorizes the person, and which serves no legitimate purpose. The course of

conduct must be such as would cause a reasonable person to suffer substantial emotional distress, and must actually cause substantial emotional distress to the person.

115. Ibid.

116. Cal. Civ. Code §1708.7 (3)(A)(2018). "…the plaintiff must have, on at least one occasion, clearly and definitely demanded that the defendant cease and abate his or her pattern of conduct and the defendant persisted in his or her pattern of conduct…"

117. Cal. Const. Art. 1 §2(b).

118. *O'Grady v. Superior Court*, Cal. Ct. App. (2006).

119. Mickey Osterreicher (attorney) in discussion with author, January 2018.

120. Nicholas Schmidle, "The Digital Dirt: How TMZ Gets the Videos and Photos that Celebrities Want to Hide," *The New Yorker*, February 22, 2013, http://www.newyorker.com/magazine/2016/02/22/inside-harvey-levins-tmz.

121. Ibid.

122. *Raef v. Superior Court*, 240 Cal. App. 4th 1112 (2015).

123. FAA UAS Symposium, Local and State UAS Enforcement Authorities, March 27, 2017, https://www.faa.gov/uas/resources/events_calendar/archive/2017_uas_symposium/media/Workshop_7_Local_and_State_UAS_Enforcement_Authorities.pdf.

FOUR

Interviews with Paparazzi about California's Privacy and Anti-Harassment Laws

While dozens of paparazzi work across Los Angeles, many declined to be interviewed on the record for this book; however, a handful, twelve, agreed. Additionally, three paparazzi agreed to extensive in-depth interviews and gave permission to be identified by name. This chapter analyzes what the paparazzi say about how California's privacy and anti-harassment laws have impacted their profession. It concludes with a discussion of how some individual photographers entered the celebrity-focused photography business.

ARE THE PRIVACY AND ANTI-HARASSMENT LAWS SUCCESSFUL?

The following questions were asked of twelve photographers to determine if and how the two anti-paparazzi laws impacted their careers. These questions included their professional ethics codes, whether celebrity privacy is possible in Los Angeles, and if the First Amendment's Freedom of Press rights should include them. The paparazzi's answers provide unique insight by those at the center of the state government's efforts to protect celebrities' private lives. The following questions were asked:

1. How has the California privacy law aimed at paparazzi changed your professional behavior?
2. Do you believe the privacy law is effective in protecting celebrity privacy? Why or why not?

3. Have you ever been accused of following or monitoring celebrities under California's anti-harassment state law? If so, how did you react?
4. Have you ever been accused of violating a celebrity's privacy under the state law? If yes, what was your response?
5. Do you follow an ethics code in your profession?
6. How can a celebrity live a normal life here in Hollywood and avoid paparazzi?
7. Is it true that all or most celebrities know the paparazzi locations and can avoid them if they want?
8. Do you believe that paparazzi activity is protected by the First Amendment's Freedom of the Press clause?

METHODOLOGY OF RESEARCH

A former celebrity photographer helped recruit paparazzi to be interviewed. A retired TMZ field producer initially assisted in recruiting a few photographers to answer the questions. In Los Angeles, most photographers know one another or of each other by reputation. The competition for photos among them is intense. The former TMZ field producer, who asked to remain anonymous, has friends among the photographers. Yet, there were some who did not associate with him due to professional rivalry. Those who did not trust him, in turn, were predisposed to not answer questions for this book. Others would not formally answer the questions but would talk off the record. Those informal answers are not a part of this chapter's analysis and discussion.

The interviews were conducted on the streets of Beverly Hills, West Hollywood, and Los Angeles at locations where the paparazzi often gather to snap celebrity photographs. These settings included restaurants, a farmers market, the *Jimmy Kimmel Live!* studio, and in city-wide drives (photographers who drive around looking for celebrities). Only men were interviewed simply because no women photographers were seen working and therefore not approached for an interview. Most paparazzi work as freelance photographers, TMZ field producers, or directly for media agencies who, in turn, sell the visuals to magazines, websites, or entertainment television shows.

PAPARAZZI SPEAK FOR THEMSELVES

In answering the first interview question, *how has the California privacy law changed the photographers' behavior*, nearly all replied that it has *not* impacted how they conduct their jobs. Most indicated they do not photograph children or try to sneak onto a celebrity's property. One photographer admitted he will take a photograph of a child with the parent if they are out in public and *only* if the child is part of the "context" for the story, meaning they are at a family-friendly location such as an amusement park. One paparazzo stated that the law influenced media companies to change their own internal rules for how their photographers take photos. Several paparazzi connected the origins of the law to three celebrities: Jennifer Garner, Halle Berry, and Kristen Bell. In 2013, both Garner and Berry appeared before a California Assembly committee in support of the law; whereas, Bell, in 2014, led a campaign on Twitter to pressure media companies to no longer use minors' images.

While Section 1708.8 of the Civil Code, the privacy law, has kept many photographers from snapping photos of children, many stated the law is not enforced by local police authorities. Not one of them heard of a single prosecution. In fact, one photographer stated that they all "thought it would, but it had no bearing. We were waiting for someone to get in trouble." Another emphatically said there is a "certain lawlessness out here." For example, Los Angeles Airport authorities are not stopping the paparazzi from "mobbing" celebrities at the baggage claim areas. Local police are not enforcing crowd control at Beverly Hills restaurants. Another photographer said despite the overall intention of the law, "We still do the same. We go out there and they [celebrities] are not going to call the cops." As an example, Beverly Hills Police Department officers do not interfere with photographers who gather in front of Craig's restaurant in Beverly Hills each night waiting to take photos. Another photographer said, "It's the Wild West out here" in reference to a lack of police monitoring large gatherings of paparazzi.

About half of those interviewed answered the question, *have you ever been accused of violating a celebrity's privacy under the state law,* admitting that celebrities have become angry at them for violating their privacy, but they were quick to point out they were always working in a public venue. Those who said they were accused by a celebrity of violating their privacy, the police were never notified. One said that actress Natalie Portman shouted at him as he photographed her hiking with a friend, and another paparazzo said that Bruce Willis became angry when his photograph was taken at a public park in Beverly Hills where he was playing outside with his children.

When the photographers were asked if they had ever been accused of *harassing a celebrity* in violation of Section 1708.7 of the Civil Code, most answered no. The two respondents who said yes, qualified their answers. One paparazzo said that he simply told the celebrity that he was not violating the anti-harassment law, and he continued to take photos. Another respondent answered that he tried to explain that he needed the celebrity's photos. Instead of taking a photo at a particular moment, several paparazzi noted that in the past they arranged other opportunities to meet a celebrity. Most paparazzi said many celebrities understand this is a business, and while they may not want to have their photo taken at a particular moment, many are willing to accommodate a photographer in order to get the publicity. Another paparazzo explained that he negotiated with Halle Berry's publicist not to photograph the Oscar winner after an appearance on the *Jimmy Kimmel Live!* show in exchange for an alternate time and venue.

While nearly all respondents said they do not harass their subjects, ironically half of them answered yes to the question *whether paparazzi photography is a form of harassment toward celebrities*. There is a general belief among paparazzi that *other photographers* (their competition) do cross a line and openly harass their intended subjects. They are quick to blame their competitors and provided answers such as, "In some circumstances, it is false imprisonment and they [celebrity] can't move"; "It depends how you do your job"; and "Take your photo and move on. You don't need lots of photos of the same thing." One respondent was emphatic in his belief that his job is not a form of harassment under any circumstance, stating, "They chose to be a celebrity." He said that by becoming a public personality, the consequences include having their photo taken anytime, anywhere. This echoes what famous paparazzo Ron Galella said in a 2014 interview, "If celebrities want privacy, they should stay home. They should expect paparazzi in public."[1]

Paparazzi were asked if they *follow an ethics code*. Nearly all respondents answered they do have personal codes of ethics they follow. None spoke about the codes of ethics from journalism organizations such as Society of Professional Journalists or Radio Television Digital News Association. All respondents but one indicated they do not take photos of minors. If the privacy law has made any impact on this profession, it is in this area. Most celebrity photographers are adamant about not taking photos of children unless they have the permission of the parent. While photographing celebrities' children is rare, it still occurs. In May 2018, Kristen Bell openly confronted a photographer who was sitting in his car and taking photos of her picking up her children at school.[2] He had photos of both Bell and her children.

One respondent answered the ethics question by stating, "I never harass and never elicit a response from a mean question." The term *mean question* means a photographer approaching a celebrity in a confrontational manner to record an angry or outrageous response that places the celebrity in a negative light. Another paparazzo said, "I don't house-sit or chase." House-sit literally means waiting outside celebrities' houses to take photos when they leave and then possibly following them by car for more visuals. Another said he acts professionally all the time and his approach is "do as little harm as possible," but he did not elaborate. A few respondents said that if a celebrity becomes agitated when they are photographed, they may then erase the photos if they are given another opportunity at a later time to shoot that same person. Two photographers admitted to taking money for putting the camera away. They said the money was often the same amount as what they probably would have earned selling the photo.

The variety of answers about photographers' individual code of ethics is not surprising. Pascal Rostain, a famous paparazzo, said in 2014 that ethics "are fixed by a baseline of decency."[3] His colleague, Francis Apesteguy in the same interview, answered, "Each person has their own limits."[4] Sebastien Valiela's perspective on ethics reflects the answers from the twelve photographers interviewed, "There is no obviously written code of ethics. Everyone does as they choose."[5]

When asked *if celebrities can live private lives in and around Los Angeles*, most indicated that celebrities know how to live a somewhat normal life away from the cameras. Photographers often added that avoiding Beverly Hills, Hollywood, West Hollywood, and Studio City would help maintain privacy. A few said that if celebrities do not want to encounter paparazzi, they should live in the Los Angeles suburbs of Pasadena and Santa Barbara. All the photographers said that the paparazzi hotspots are known and no celebrity can plead ignorance about this. The paparazzi, as a group, do not hide their presence at restaurants such as Craig's, Madeo, and Mr. Chow. During the week they walk up and down the sidewalks of Beverly Hills, especially on Canon Drive, where several restaurants have outdoor seating. On Sundays the paparazzi will be combing local farmers markets, including one in Studio City where celebrities are known to shop.

Of course, living a normal life is relative to each person. But if a celebrity simply does not want the glare of the camera lens, then they can mostly avoid it. This does not mean paparazzi only work in Beverly Hills, Studio City, or Hollywood. They do work across Los Angeles, but the farther any celebrity is away from the epicenter, while not a guarantee, the more likely they are to have a private life.

All respondents were quick to point out that one of the secrets of the entire business is the publicists who discreetly call or message media companies or specific photographers telling them where a celebrity will be at a specific time. All the photographers said that celebrities excel at prearranging their photos in this discreet way. They said this was the irony to their job. They are hated by many celebrities until that celebrity needs publicity. Few, if any, paparazzi or stars will turn down this exclusive opportunity.

With the last question, *do you believe that paparazzi are protected by the First Amendment's Freedom of the Press clause*, the unanimous answer was yes. The respondents' reasons varied, but they all believe their profession is a form of journalism. One paparazzo said, "What we are doing is news. It is no different than sports or real estate reporting. It is journalism, soft news." They agree that the exception to freedom of the press is in the rare circumstance that a photographer invades someone's property in person or with a telephoto lens. One paparazzo went further and advocated that they are the "only real journalists in L.A." because of the American public's fascination with celebrities' lives. They all said they are responding to the public's desire to see celebrities, and paparazzi provide that product as journalism.

Since most paparazzi said they perform their jobs on public property, they are protected under state law. The security coordinator for the weekly Sunday Studio City Farmers Market agreed with that assessment.[6] He said the only times he objects to photographers' activities is when he receives complaints they interfere with the other customers' shopping, or they photograph children without permission. Echoing what paparazzi said, the security coordinator stated the streets and sidewalks across Los Angeles are public property and can be used by photographers.

Chapter 6 discusses how the two California laws impact paparazzi First Amendment rights. Paparazzi abilities to photograph celebrities is a form of free press. They all strongly advocate for this right even if the public does not respect their profession. As discussed in chapter 2, both legal experts Mickey Osterriecher and Frank LoMonte agree with this basic First Amendment right. Their role as journalists is fundamental to freedom of the press.

PROFILES OF THREE CELEBRITY PHOTOGRAPHERS

In addition to the twelve paparazzi surveyed, three were further interviewed in detail about the laws' impact on the industry and their own careers. They provided an unparalleled inside perspective of the profession including how they started in the business. They provided unique insight on how paparazzi earn a living. They also opened up about their own roles within the profession including their personal codes of ethics.

Jennifer Buhl, one of a small handful of former women paparazzi, worked as a photographer between 2006 and 2009. She moved to Los Angeles in 2005 to work in television but ended up paying her bills by working at a coffee shop.[7] She said that one day a few paparazzi came in to buy coffee and told her about their job: "It was one of those light bulb moments where this is what I want to be doing now in my life."[8] She had worked previous jobs in television entertainment and news including CNN in Atlanta, Georgia.

Giles Harrison has worked as a paparazzo for more than twenty-five years and entered the business from a career producing and selling celebrity video interviews to television shows such as *Access Hollywood* and *Inside Edition*. He indicated that in a few years he expects to no longer drive around Los Angeles five days a week and take photos. In his twenty-five years as a paparazzo, he experienced the economic highs and lows of the business.

Vince Flores, a former fifteen-year paparazzo veteran, worked at a Wells Fargo bank and enrolled in digital photography editing classes. A bank client he knew offered him a part-time job teaching Adobe Photoshop to adult students. That job, in turn, led to an offer of taking photos on the red carpet at the Emmys. He sent those photos electronically to Startraks Photo Agency, and more opportunities came his way. Flores photographed celebrities at red carpet events, including awards shows and movie premieres, and he earned money driving around Los Angeles taking photos.[9]

When asked if paparazzi photography is a form of journalism, both Harrison and Flores consider themselves first and foremost as photojournalists. They believe they work in entertainment news. In fact, Harrison is emphatic about how he defines his profession: "I consider myself a journalist first and a photographer second."[10] While most of his work is as a celebrity photographer, he also covers hard, breaking news. He believes that celebrity journalism is equal to hard news and that he is as legitimate a reporter as someone covering sports or any other beat: "We are supplying a product, we are supplying photos for news stories and we have clients and that's what they buy and so there is a demand and we provide it."[11] While celebrity news may be the "lighter, fluffier part of news," Harrison believes his work is no less important than the work journalists have in covering nationals and world leaders.[12] He strongly believes the First Amendment guarantees his right to work as a paparazzo.

Flores agrees with Harrison's view about the legitimacy of celebrity news as a form of journalism. A typical day for Flores included any number of opportunities to take photos including ribbon cutting ceremonies, red carpet events, or movie premieres. He described a typical busy day from April 2018:

> My day consisted of Lynda Carter getting a star on Hollywood Walk of Fame and that ended at 12:30 to 1 p.m. Then I drove around Los Angeles and I found Selena Gomez at the gym she goes to so I shot her walking out of the gym and then I drove around again and found Paris Hilton's car. I shot Paris Hilton coming out of a cosmetics store and then I went to a movie premiere that I was invited to.[13]

On any given day, Flores might attend a celebrity event later featured on the evening news, but also photograph a celebrity at a restaurant and that image later appeared in a tabloid magazine. Both Flores and Harrison argue that whether it's a Hollywood Walk of Fame celebrity event, movie premiere, or a photo of a celebrity out and about in Los Angeles, these are all legitimate journalism stories. The public has a right to read about them.

Former paparazza Jennifer Buhl did consider herself a photojournalist but was also comfortable with a distinction between photojournalist and paparazzi. She did not consider herself an entertainment or celebrity journalist, but instead a "tabloid journalist."[14] This view parallels Kim McNamara's study of the origins of American paparazzi. She noted that in the 1970s "serious" photojournalism was not as important as tabloid-related photography.[15] McNamara found that it was easier for newsrooms to cover celebrity gossip rather than hard news. The safe move for photographers was to have a celebrity beat instead of the traditional war- and crime-based investigative journalism.[16] For many photographers, celebrity photos were not only safer but more lucrative forms of work. From Buhl's perspective, her celebrity photo beat was secondary to other beats such as breaking news and sports: "something that wasn't as important to the world except in the form of entertainment."[17] Yet, she still claimed the title journalist as part of her career.

Even famed paparazzo Ron Galella, who spent years following Jackie Kennedy Onassis in New York City, considered himself a journalist.[18] Los Angeles paparazzo Rick Mendoza prefers to call himself a "candid street celebrity photographer."[19] He argued that paparazzi record events through photography: "Journalism is recording the story. It's history."[20] Yet, even as a street celebrity photographer, his photos have appeared in mainstream magazines such as *Cosmopolitan* and *New York* and also online, where many paparazzi photos appear.[21] The belief that paparazzi photography is a form of journalism is one that Kim McNamara's research into media agencies supports.[22] Media agencies that buy photos from paparazzi believe the work is a form of journalism.[23]

PAPARAZZI ETHICS

If the paparazzi interviewed for this book believe they are working journalists who specialize in celebrity photos, an important question asked of Harrison, Flores, and Buhl was what ethics guided them in their jobs. Paparazzi are often reviled by both the public and celebrities, but they supply the visual product published in magazines and websites. The public disgust peaked in 1997, when Princess Diana was killed in the tragic Paris car accident. As discussed in chapter 2, many professional journalism organizations have codes of ethics for the print, broadcast, or photography journalism, and the twelve street-based paparazzi, discussed in this chapter had their own personal ethical compasses. Harrison, Flores, and Buhl all stated they conducted their jobs with integrity based on an ethical core.

Specifically, Buhl noted that for her and other paparazzi, the biggest obstacle to getting photos some days was "your own moral conscience."[24] There were times she passed on a photo of a celebrity so she would not be personally embarrassed in a public place:

> While you can legally go into a grocery store, restaurant, a hotel, or a public place and photograph until you are asked to leave and which

> case you legally have to leave, but you are allowed to do that and really, you don't do that very frequently. Maybe it's moral, it's that internal you don't want to get embarrassed, you don't want to embarrass them [celebrity], you don't want to call attention to yourself.[25]

Buhl admitted that this can happen up to 75 percent of the time when tracking a celebrity at an indoor, private business. Her own ethics steered away from these locations. Often, she sat in her car and tried to be discreet waiting for celebrities to go outside and then shoot them.[26] She also tried to approach them respectfully: "I wouldn't be a jerk to the celebrity. I wouldn't heckle them. I wouldn't say mean things."[27] She found that heckling and mocking celebrities only led them to cover their faces, depriving her and other paparazzi of any photograph.

Fifteen-year paparazzo veteran Vince Flores tried to cultivate a somewhat personal and respectful relationship with celebrities. His approach to the job was about obtaining a certain number of photos per day that he could sell to Startracks Photo Agency. Beyond that quota, if a celebrity asked him to refrain from a photo, he considered their request:

> It depends on the celebrity. I mean obviously I have to get photos. . . . Jennifer Garner is cordial. So, if she was to tell me "I don't want any photos" I won't do it. But if she were to tell me that every day? No.[28]

In some cases, if he noticed a celebrity having a bad day and seemed upset for some reason, he simply may not take the picture:

> There was one time I was shooting Emily Ratajkowski [on election day] . . . and she was Instagram savvy about how she feels about politics and everything. So, I went to her voting booth [location] and I papped (photographed) her coming out. . . . I'm not sure what happened that day but she was extremely upset so when she got out, she was rubbing her eyes and it was obvious to me that she was upset. She walked over to my car and she told me, "please don't take my photograph today." She was like "delete them" and I did it and the reason I did it was because when she sees me she realizes, "hey if I just give this guy a picture, he's going to leave me alone."[29]

Flores believed that when he respected a celebrity's request from time to time, he built a level of trust with them, cultivating a professional work relationship: "I think everyone understands we need each other. I need them as much as they need me."[30] This symbiotic need is what nearly all paparazzi pointed to in defending their profession.

Twenty-five-year paparazzo veteran Giles Harrison explained that in the beginning of his career he would "lurk" around looking for celebrities, but he said that approach didn't seem ethical. He prefers to "give people their space."[31] His approach to the job is to take photos when celebrities do not know they are even being photographed in and around Los Angeles. Similar to Flores, Harrison tries to collect a certain number of photos per day so that he can then respect a celebrity who may ask him at a later time not to take their photo. He is adamant that respect and politeness guide his interactions: "I just try to keep it within the bounds of human respect and politeness."[32] Harrison readily admits there are paparazzi who are "ruthless" in their job, often because they work for agencies who want photos at all costs even if that means offending the celebrity.[33]

All three paparazzi, Jennifer Buhl, Vince Flores, and Giles Harrison, explicitly point out that celebrities can live in Los Angeles in relative privacy similar to what the twelve other photographers said. It is no secret which restaurants and hotels are frequented by paparazzi looking for photos. The celebrities who travel in entourages and are accompanied by security guards are the ones who are highly sought after. A celebrity's value often increases when there is a change in their personal life such as a marriage, divorce, or pregnancy.

WORKING WITHIN THE BOUNDS OF THE FIRST AMENDMENT

Since most paparazzi believe they are working journalists and follow a personal core of ethics, they also believe the First Amendment freedom of the press clause protects their rights as photographers. Buhl, Flores, and Harrison are adamant that they never broke any federal or state privacy laws. Positioning themselves as journalists means freedom of the press applies to them as much as any other reporter. When asked if the First Amendment protects his rights as a paparazzo photographer, Vince Flores succinctly stated: "As long as I am abiding by the laws and not breaking the laws, absolutely."[34] The tougher question for all three is whether California's privacy and anti-harassment laws, as discussed in chapter 3, are an effective tool in protecting celebrities' privacy and deterring paparazzi. Flores believes that Section 1707.8 of the California civil code is about protecting the celebrities' families: "You don't want the child to feel threatened, so that's the law."[35] Minors are not the sole focus of the law. It actually encompasses any activity conducted by the paparazzi on someone's personal property where any property owner including a celebrity has a reasonable expectation of privacy. Prince Harry and his wife, Meghan Markle, argue that very point. They expect family privacy in and around the property of their Santa Barbara home.[36]

Giles Harrison argues that celebrities and their children are *not* chased by packs of photographers.[37] That is simply a misconception. He argued that paparazzi who follow children are so few and far in number, that existing laws prior to 2014 could have been used to prosecute them. Harrison warned that creating laws to target any professional group that is protected under the First Amendment is dangerous, calling it a "slippery slope" to censorship.[38]

According to Buhl, Harrison, and Flores, the part of Section 1707.8 that prohibits the use of advanced technology including drones as a means to invade privacy was a needless addition.[39] None of them knows of any paparazzi who ever used a drone to conduct their work. As with the anti-privacy laws, Harrison stated that existing trespassing laws would apply to drones: "People have a reasonable expectation of privacy and you send a drone over their house. That's a problem. Just like if you are in a helicopter over their house, that would be a problem."[40] He says the 2014 laws, as a whole, were a deterrent to behavior, but have not been successful in changing any paparazzi behavior since most of them were working within state laws. As other paparazzi mentioned, there are always those few photographers who will go to *any* means (including illegal) for a photo, but those individuals are few and far between at this point.

CELEBRITIES CAN LIVE A PRIVATE LIFE (MOSTLY)

The three paparazzi all believe that despite the laws' intent of providing more privacy for celebrities and their families, celebrities can have lives where they are rarely hounded by photographers. Vince Flores noted that it is easier to live in relative obscurity in Los Angeles than in New York City. He said they are able to live in gated communities, where the public needs permission to enter, as opposed to New York City, where a celebrity may leave their front "doorstep and you are on the street" with photographers waiting for you.[41] Harrison said that many celebrities live in Los Angeles and have a private life where they are not followed by the paparazzi. Celebrities know which restaurants in areas around Los Angeles are frequented by paparazzi. Those who do not want to be exposed can avoid those areas. Jennifer Buhl cited the example of how Britney Spears moved from the tabloid pages to being left alone:

> Britney Spears was really hot when I was a paparazzi [2006–2009]. She shaved her head, and she was acting crazy every day. Every day there were loads of paparazzi hanging outside her house because they knew she was going to come out and do something wacky and the tabloids were going to talk about it. Now, I don't know anybody who works on Britney Spears. She decided that's not how she wants to live.[42]

The case of Britney Spears is interesting. While the paparazzi had intense interest in her for several years, they gradually stopped following her as her life became more private. For many years, Spears remained below the public's radar and then started using Instagram in summer 2019 to gain notoriety for her fitness routine. She posted numerous photos of herself exercising with her boyfriend. Those photos were often published by the media. Spears is actively increasing her media presence.

As noted in chapter 1 of this book, Jennifer Aniston complained in 2016 in a *Huffington Post* essay about paparazzi hounding her outside her home.[43] All three paparazzi dispute that photographers surround her home on a daily basis. Jennifer Buhl said that one time in 2007 she took a photo of Aniston walking on the beach and she earned $100 for it.[44] That $100 reflected a low value for an Aniston photo since she had not been in the tabloids for some time. Buhl stated that when Aniston had a life-changing event, such as the 2018 divorce from Justin Theroux, her tabloid profile changed, causing an increase in the value of her photo. In those instances, Buhl agrees that paparazzi may then be standing outside her home. But on a daily basis, the paparazzi are not waiting outside for her.[45] Harrison put it more directly about Aniston's claim that paparazzi surround and hound her:

> I think what most people forget about her is that nine times out of ten when people are pursuing her, it's a story surrounding her. She is breaking up with her husband or who she is going out with. With people like Jennifer Aniston, it's not like she has a hit movie. It's not like she's the biggest movie star in the world. What make her interesting to publications is her personal life and the fact that, yeah, she is not photographed that often. She's *not* going to be photographed like everyone else shopping around, that's not happening.[46]

Harrison also noted the irony that the other former cast members from *Friends,* including Courtney Cox and Lisa Kudrow, lead relatively private lives in comparison to Aniston. They made a decision years ago to live their lives quietly away from the cameras.

The actors, musicians, and reality stars who want to have their photos published in magazines and the online tabloids allow themselves to be photographed. So-called B-list celebrities become less valuable the more they live private lives, even in the Los Angeles area. Buhl explained that certain celebrities use the paparazzi to increase their own value within the entertainment industry, and the paparazzi are happy to oblige with photos that will get published. Buhl, Harrison, and Flores all agreed that the celebrity photo business comes down to an issue of many of the celebrities needing the photographers and the paparazzi know it. They all recognized the irony of any celebrity complaining about the paparazzi one day and then on another day wanting their photo taken to promote an upcoming television show or movie.

LIVES OF THE PAPARAZZI

Buhl, Harrison, and Flores never aspired to be a part of the paparazzi profession. As discussed earlier in this chapter, it happened by accident. Most did not have childhood ambitions to live in Los Angeles and follow celebrities around capturing their photos. Many, such as Buhl and Harrison, studied journalism or photography in college and entered the paparazzi field when they first moved to Los Angeles to find media jobs. The lure of a high paycheck in the late 1990s or early 2000s was too much to resist. Living in Los Angeles is expensive. Rent and gasoline prices are among the highest in United States. Often, paparazzi simply fell into the job by meeting photographers working their celebrity beats. They are easy to find, especially at restaurants and at the premieres and red carpet events.

There is no formal training to become a paparazzo, nor is there an internship or mentoring program. Several photographers interviewed for this book believe the industry no longer embraces photography as an art or journalism skill. In the age of digital cameras, it is simply literally clicking on the camera dozens of times hoping that one photo is the good one for publication. The paparazzi business is intense and not for the lazy. It is a physical grind tracking down celebrities and waiting for them to appear. Former paparazza Jennifer Buhl called it a "very aggressive" job with lots of boredom but also packed with adrenaline.[47] Paparazzo Rick Mendoza said that the job requires photographers to think fast and not hesitate to take photos.[48] Patience is an important part of the job until that moment arrives when the paparazzo takes *the* photo of a Selena Gomez, Kardashian family member, or rapper Machine Gun Kelly. The competition among those paparazzi is tough. According to Jennifer McNamara, "many will have to jostle with other paparazzi to take what are effectively identical shots of a celebrity."[49]

Each paparazzo needs to have a standard number of photos each week to earn a base level of income.[50] An unobstructed photo of a celebrity may be considered an exclusive and if that celebrity is in high demand that week, the photo could be worth thousands of dollars.[51] Often that high-valued photo is from sheer luck of where the photographer was standing since there could be dozens of paparazzi surrounding a celebrity. Paparazzi are known to bully each other for the best camera position to take a photo and often need to stay in place for hours at a time to wait for that one photo, especially at a red carpet event. The competition for the highly valued photograph is fierce. The work continues rain or shine, in the summer heat or winter's cooler temperatures.

The photographers interviewed for this chapter estimate there are fewer than one hundred paparazzi across Los Angeles and most of them are men. Jennifer Buhl estimated less than a dozen photographers are women.[52] They are out in the field working days or nights driving around Los Angeles trying to find celebrities' cars, waiting for tips on celebrity locations, or standing outside well-known restaurants or coffee shops and the airport. From day to day the money earned can increase or go down, and they never quite know how much money they will earn for their photos. Just as a company's stock goes up and down on the New York Stock Exchange, a celebrity's photographic value can change daily or monthly.[53] The media agencies that buy the photos tell the paparazzi which celebrities' "stock" is up on a particular day. Those with a high value are intently pursued.

FINAL PERSPECTIVES ON THE PAPARAZZO'S CAREER

As conveyed by the interviews and in-depth conversations discussed in this chapter, the job of paparazzo is not an easy one. The money earned is not consistent. While most paparazzi stated that the privacy and anti-harassment laws have not impacted their careers, they are, nonetheless, actively aware of the state government's intent to protect celebrity's privacy. They are keenly aware the authorities could be called even if it is unlikely.

Whether or not the law is actively enforced by local police authorities is not as relevant as the fact that many paparazzi are watching their conduct for fear of prosecution. They consciously stay in public areas where they can take photos. While they may not be legal experts, they know enough not to cross privacy boundaries, including physically preventing their celebrity subjects from walking or driving. All those interviewed stressed that their jobs are a form of journalism and protected by the First Amendment. Yet, most admit they simply will not go to *any* means to acquire a photo. Those methods include taking photos of children, staking out homes, or openly harassing the celebrity. Increasingly, paparazzi know their legal rights and actively stay away from violating Sections 1708.7 and 1708.8 of the state's Civil Code.

In addition to paparazzi ensuring they are not harassing a celebrity, there are the added financial and physical stresses of the job. They never know from day to day which, if any, celebrity they will photograph and if that photo will be worth a substantial amount of money. Working a twelve- to fifteen-hour shift combing the streets and restaurants for photographs is never a guarantee of a high payout. There are always two factors to consider on a daily basis: whether a celebrity sighting will occur *and* if it does, how much money that paparazzo will earn from that photo. Those two factors are constant in a paparazzo's life but are both riddled with inconsistency.

NOTES

1. Clement Cheroux, Camille Lenglois, Vera Leon, and Max Bonhomme, "Hazards of the Trade: Interviews with Paparazzi," in *Paparazzi! Photographers, Stars, Artists*, ed. Clement Cheroux and Alain Seban (France, Flammarion 2014).
2. Rebecca Dube, "The amazing way Kristen Bell confronted paparazzi taking photos of her children," May 6, 2018, https://www.today.com/parents/kristen-bell-confronted-paparazzi-photographing-her-children-t128440.

3. Cheroux, Lenglois, Leon, and Bonhomme, "Hazards of the Trade: Interviews with Paparazzi," 36.
4. Ibid.
5. Ibid.
6. The security manager of the Studio City Farmers Market asked not to have his identity used in this chapter.
7. Jennifer Buhl (freelance photographer) in discussion with author, April 2018.
8. Ibid.
9. Vince Flores (former Startraks Photo photographer and paparazzo) in discussion with author, April 2018.
10. Giles Harrison (owner, London Entertainment Group and paparazzo) in discussion with author, April 2018.
11. Ibid.
12. Ibid.
13. Ibid.
14. Jennifer Buhl (freelance photographer) in discussion with author, April 2018.
15. Kim McNamara, *Paparazzi: Media Practices and Celebrity Culture* (Malden, MA: Polity Press, 2016), 104.
16. Ibid.
17. Jennifer Buhl (freelance photographer) in discussion with author, April 2018.
18. Clémont Chéroux, Camille Lenglois, Véra Léon, and Max Bonhomme, "Hazards of the Trade: Interviews with Paparazzi," in *Paparazzi! Photographers, Stars, Artists* ed. Clément Chéroux (Paris: Flammarion, 2014), 36.
19. Elaine Kagan, "Confessions of a Paparazzo," *Los Angeles Magazine,* February 25, 2015, http://www.lamag.com/longform/confessions-paparazzo/.
20. Ibid.
21. Ibid.
22. Kim McNamara, *Paparazzi: Media Practices and Celebrity Culture* (Malden, MA: Polity Press, 2016), 109.
23. Ibid.
24. Jennifer Buhl (freelance photographer) in discussion with author, April 2018.
25. Ibid.
26. Ibid.
27. Ibid.
28. Vince Flores (former Startraks Photo photographer and paparazzo) in discussion with author, April 2018.
29. Ibid.
30. Ibid.
31. Giles Harrison (owner, London Entertainment Group and paparazzo) in discussion with author, April 2018.
32. Ibid.
33. Ibid
34. Vince Flores (former Startraks Photo photographer and paparazzo) in discussion with author, April 2018.
35. Ibid.
36. Cal. Civ. Code §1708.8 (1)(a) (2017). The law states "A person is liable for physical invasion of privacy when the defendant knowingly enters onto the land of another person without permission or otherwise committed a trespass in order to physically invade the privacy of the plaintiff with the intent to capture any type of visual image, sound recording, or other physical impression of the plaintiff engaging in a personal or familial activity and the physical invasion occurs in a manner that is offensive to a reasonable person."
37. Giles Harrison (owner, London Entertainment Group and paparazzo) in discussion with author, April 2018.
38. Ibid.

39. Cal. Civ. Code §1708.8 (1) (b) (2017). While not specifically mentioning the use of drone, the law infers it, "A person is liable for constructive invasion of privacy when the defendant attempts to capture, in a manner that is offensive to a reasonable person, any type of visual image, sound recording, or other physical impression of the plaintiff engaging in a personal or familial activity under circumstances in which the plaintiff had a reasonable expectation of privacy, through the use of any device, regardless of whether there is a physical trespass, if this image, sound recording, or other physical impression could not have been achieved without a trespass unless the device was used."

40. Ibid.

41. Vince Flores (former Startraks Photo photographer and paparazzo) in discussion with author, April 2018.

42. Jennifer Buhl (freelance photographer) in discussion with author, April 2018.

43. Jennifer Aniston, "For the Record," *Huffington Post*, July 12, 2016, http://www.huffingtonpost.com/entry/for-the-record_us_57855586e4b03fc3ee4e626f.

44. Jennifer Buhl (freelance photographer) in discussion with author, April 2018.

45. Ibid.

46. Giles Harrison (owner, London Entertainment Group and paparazzo) in discussion with author, April 2018.

47. Jennifer Buhl (freelance photographer) in discussion with author, April 2018.

48. Elaine Kagan, "Confessions of a Paparazzo," *Los Angeles Magazine,* February 25, 2015, http://www.lamag.com/longform/confessions-paparazzo/.

49. Kim McNamara, *Paparazzi: Media Practices and Celebrity Culture* (Malden, MA: Polity Press, 2016), 41.

50. Ibid.

51. Ibid.

52. Jennifer Buhl (freelance photographer) in discussion with author, April 2018.

53. Elaine Kagan, "Confessions of a Paparazzo," *Los Angeles Magazine,* February 25, 2015, http://www.lamag.com/longform/confessions-paparazzo/.

Actress Helen Hunt signs autographs as she leaves Craig's restaurant in Beverly Hills, CA. July 11, 2019. Photo by Joshua Azriel.

Randy Bauer of the Bauer-Griffin Photo Agency uses a telephoto lens to take photos of guests who appear on *Jimmy Kimmel Live!* July 11, 2019. Photo by Joshua Azriel.

Paparazzi line up to take a celebrity's photo. They are often told ahead of time when a celebrity is about to exit Craig's restaurant in Beverly Hills, CA. July 17, 2019. Photo by Joshua Azriel.

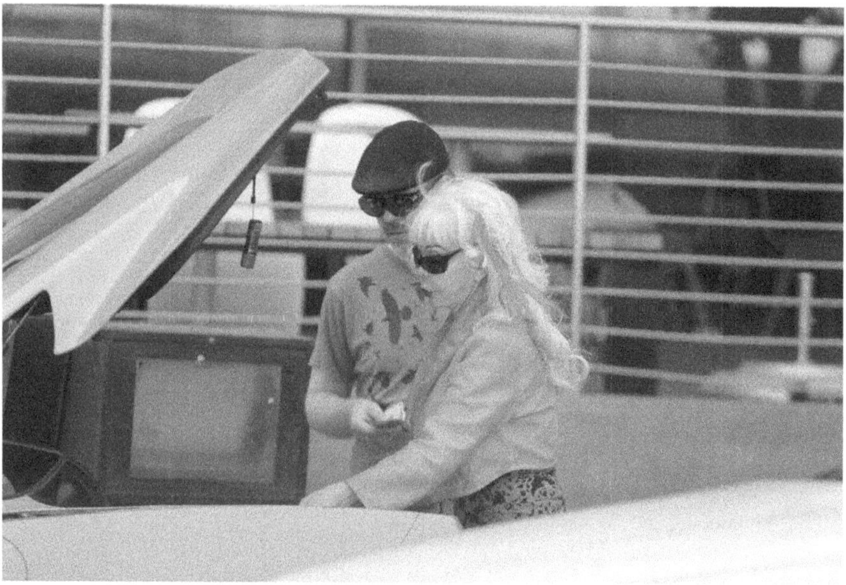

Local Los Angeles celebrity Angelyne selling her own souvenirs out of her famed pink Corvette. Angelyne is famous for her 1980s billboards that displayed her photo and telephone number as a way of promoting her acting career. July 15, 2019. Photo by Joshua Azriel.

Invited photographers stand in a designated section of the *Fast & Furious Presents: Hobbs & Shaw* movie premiere at the Dolby Theatre in Hollywood, CA. Actors from the movie and guests who are invited to the premiere event walk by this group of photographers. July 13, 2019. Photo by Joshua Azriel.

Actors Dwayne Johnson and Jason Statham, the stars of *Fast & Furious Presents: Hobbs & Shaw* surrounded by photographers at the premiere held at the Dolby Theatre in Hollywood, CA. July 13, 2019 Photo by Joshua Azriel.

Invited photographers standing in a designated section of the *Fast & Furious Presents: Hobbs & Shaw* movie premiere at the Dolby Theatre in Hollywood, CA. Actors from the movie and guests who are invited to the premiere event walk by this group of photographers for photo opportunities. July 13, 2019. Photo by Joshua Azriel.

Well-known Los Angeles publicist Elliot Mintz and his attorney Diana Fitzgerald stand for photos in front of paparazzi outside of Craig's restaurant in Beverly Hills, CA. This photo is from the perspective of a paparazzo. Mintz is known for representing celebrity clients including Paris Hilton, Paris Jackson, Bob Dylan, and Diana Ross. July 15, 2019. Photo by Joshua Azriel.

FIVE

Professional Life as a Paparazzo

This chapter regarding four different field observation experiences of paparazzi could not have been written without the assistance of a few local Los Angeles paparazzi and autograph collectors.[1] They provided valuable inside knowledge about where celebrity photographers work. Autograph collectors often stand around with paparazzi in hopes of acquiring an autograph that can be sold to collectors. They often exchange information with paparazzi about celebrity sightings at different locations. Celebrity photography and autograph collecting are highly competitive in Los Angeles, and despite assurances, they feared that the information they provided would be used by the competition to outwit them for photo opportunities. Several photographers and autograph seekers asked that their identities remain confidential in return for assisting with this research.

In order to research Los Angeles paparazzi and whether the anti-paparazzi laws discussed in this book affect the industry, it was important to embed with them. Embed meant spending a week working as a paparazzo photographer while formally and informally interviewing them. In reality, two qualitative research techniques were needed: participant observation and in-depth interviews. Both research methodologies required trusting photographers who worked in the field or who recently retired from it. These informal research partners assisted with needed introductions to others, and they were instrumental in suggesting specific locations to find paparazzi. The field research described in this chapter was only possible with the help of these individuals.

Working as a celebrity photographer is physically demanding. In order to get paid, they must take photographs and record videos each day. Weather, traffic, and personal health are no excuses for not working. Red carpet photographers stand on their feet in a restricted area for hours, and they cannot move from their position once the event starts. Other photographers literally walk the streets of Hollywood, Beverly Hills, or other areas of Los Angeles all day tracking celebrities and chasing down a confidential tip they receive. Once they acquire their photo, they move in search of the next one. A few photographers drive around the city all day and may repeatedly circle the same few blocks in Beverly Hills looking for a celebrity's car or surveying the customers at an outdoor restaurant. Still others stake out the Los Angeles airport as early at 5 a.m. and do not leave until noon or 1 p.m. Paparazzi are not lazy and work long days.

The consensus among the paparazzi is that the overall pay they earn for photos has decreased in recent years. The common phrase often heard is that they are "working twice as hard for half of the pay" from five or ten years ago. With reduced income, the levels of distrust and competition among each other has increased greatly. The decrease in earnings is directly related to celebrities posting their own photos on Instagram and other social media. As one paparazzo explained at the Studio City Farmers Market, "it's just a job," but that job is increasingly under financial pressure especially with actors, reality stars, and athletes now in control of their own publicity.

The days of violent confrontations between celebrities and photographers are mostly over. While there may be the occasional scuffle, paparazzi mainly respect celebrities' personal space. They believe their industry is under attack from both celebrities who openly request privacy for their families and the economic downturn from lower prices earned from their photographs. Paparazzi are quick to remind whoever will listen that they not only have a First Amendment right to perform their job on public property, but many celebrities still need them for publicity. They are adamant that the criticism directed toward them is unfair and argue that most actors, producers, directors, and athletes know where they hang out waiting to snap a photo.

Paparazzi simply do not agree with the argument that anyone who openly works in the entertainment industry should be able to walk, drive, and dine with an expectation of privacy. These same people all know where the paparazzi hotspots are located. Photographers also point out that many publicists tip them off, especially when a celebrity wants to communicate a new romantic relationship or indirectly promote a new movie or television show. According to one security specialist in entertainment, there is still a "wag the dog" syndrome of celebrity-paparazzi relationships.[2] Over the years, Tom Cruise, Paris Hilton, Kevin Spacey, the entire Kardashian family, and others used the paparazzi to communicate a message to the public by making themselves available for photos.[3]

In the era before Instagram and other social media, celebrities *needed* paparazzi for publicity. In the age of social media, more and more celebrities are bypassing paparazzi by amassing hundreds of thousands or millions of public followers. There is a major transition underway in how celebrities communicate. Paparazzi know this and are working twice as hard for fewer dollars than they were a decade ago. An image they may have sold for thousands of dollars may only be worth a fraction of that amount. Today, they hustle to earn a living. No one knows how many of them are working in and around Los Angeles. Estimates range from forty to nearly one hundred paparazzi who work either full- or part-time.[4]

Most paparazzi will not talk openly (on the record) about California's privacy and anti-harassment laws and how it has affected their business. Those who work for TMZ sign non-disclosure agreements and simply refuse to talk.[5] Yet, quietly off the record many stated that the laws are not enforced. The anti-harassment and privacy laws, sections 1708.7 and 1708.8 of the civil code, were passed by the California State Assembly to appease celebrities with children such as Jennifer Garner and Halle Berry, but in reality, it has not impacted how paparazzi perform their jobs. Police do not walk the streets of Beverly Hills monitoring the paparazzi. Many said the lack of law enforcement is like the "wild west." Paparazzi quietly admit they do respect and avoid photographing celebrities' families (spouses and children) since the laws have only emphasized that specific issue. Yet, not one person interviewed on or off the record for this book knows of any example where a celebrity reported an incident to the police. Aside from not taking photos of children, nearly all paparazzi indicated the laws have not changed their overall professional behavior.

This chapter discusses four typical ways paparazzi do their jobs. These methods are based on this author's firsthand experience and knowledge working with cooperative paparazzi and security experts. Regardless of the chosen method, paparazzi know there is always risk on any day of not obtaining good quality photos or getting paid.

THE STAKEOUT

Staking out multiple locations during the day is physically hard work. Paparazzi are on their feet rain or shine. A paparazzo can easily work a fifteen- to eighteen-hour day. After a day's work, the freelance photographer uploads photos to a website so agencies can bid on them. If he or she works directly for a media agency, the photographer sends the images electronically to the employer. TMZ field producers simply upload their videos to story editors, who then use them for television or post online.

The number of paparazzi working the streets is declining. As one photographer stated, it can "eat at your soul."[6] Most paparazzi know one another or know of one another. They distrust strangers and anyone they judge as their competition. Paparazzi constantly chase the exclusive photo and only cooperate with others they trust. It is a tight circle or clique of trust. They are competing in a rapidly shrinking marketplace.

Today, there are fewer celebrities whose photos bring top dollar by print and online publications than a decade ago.[7] Entertainment television shows and websites now access celebrity Instagram accounts and produce stories from them. It saves money to access free social media content produced by celebrities.

There are locations in Beverly Hills and Hollywood where celebrities, producers, and directors eat lunch and dinner. Many of these restaurants have both indoor and outdoor seating. Il Pastaio, Craig's, and Mr. Chow are three restaurants out of several where paparazzi often congregate. If someone working in the industry wants to "be seen," these are the type of restaurants they frequent. It is easy for a photographer to use a telephoto lens to capture an image of someone sitting outside and eating. Outdoor restaurants also make it easy for any photographer to literally walk by a table adjacent to the sidewalk and grab a quick photo. The subject of the photo may not even be aware of the photographer at these moments.

While they stand nearby within view of the restaurants, paparazzi do not interfere with the businesses' operations or flow of customer traffic. Several photographers indicated that if a celebrity eats at one of these establishments, then they know there is a chance they will be photographed. It's that simple. As already noted, there is no guess by anyone working in Hollywood as to where the paparazzi may be. It is easy to generate publicity buzz since the photographers are eager to snap a photo.

Paparazzi not only stand at these locations, but they work in tandem with nearby colleagues who often work for the same media company. For example, on one July 2019 afternoon, several paparazzi stayed in constant communication as they tracked Sylvester Stallone's whereabouts in Beverly Hills. TMZ had several field producers and videographers walking and driving around Beverly Hills and Hollywood communicating with one another. A photo or video of Stallone is a big opportunity to earn money. In their quest to find him, several paparazzi cooperated with autograph seekers on his whereabouts. Sadly, for the paparazzi, they were not able to find Stallone.

The two cities are adjacent to one other in metropolitan Los Angeles and sending a crew to an event or unexpected celebrity sighting is easy. Texts, phone calls, and quick drive-by conversations are used to communicate updates throughout the day. TMZ produces a daily television show and continuously updates its website; therefore, it has photographers combing Los Angeles all day.

This is an example of a paparazzi routine: each Friday legendary comedian and former movie director Mel Brooks eats at Porto Vio on Canon Drive in Beverly Hills. Celebrity photographers and autograph collectors know this. He typically arrives for lunch between 1 and 2 p.m. The photographers gather across the street and wait for him to finish eating.

As he leaves the restaurant, he is approached for photos and autographs. Autograph seekers and photographers give each other updates on whether or not Brooks arrived and even which table he may be eating at if he is visible from the street. They will informally gather in a line across the street from Porto Vio and wait for him. There is never a guarantee he will pose for a photo or sign an autograph, but they all know this is his Friday routine. If it doesn't work out one Friday, they can just try again one week later.

Another example is Craig's restaurant located on Melrose Avenue in West Hollywood. This restaurant opens daily at 5 p.m. Paparazzi know that celebrities frequently dine there Monday through Thursday evenings. The photographers gather at 5 p.m. and will stay until midnight or 1 a.m. There may be up to a dozen paparazzi waiting outside Craig's. They photograph the well-known customers arriving and leaving the restaurant. TMZ has a videographer there nearly every day. If a director, producer, athlete, or actor does not want their photo taken, they can simply avoid Craig's. Oftentimes, the photographers will literally be standing eight to ten feet in front of the restaurant's front door as a group with their cameras at the ready. In some instances, the celebrity's assistant or representative exits Craig's a few minutes ahead of their client and quietly tells a photographer to get into position. Once they leave the restaurant, the paparazzi snap the photos and record videos. At the end of the evening, they upload the images. This routine is repeated at other local restaurants such as Mr. Chow and Madeo.

In some cases, celebrities or their teams inform the paparazzi ahead of time where they will be. For example, on Wednesday, July 10, 2019, Kim Kardashian and her husband, Kanye West, dined at Craig's for dinner. There was a large number of photographers waiting for her. Unlike most other customers who are dropped off ten feet from the front door, Kim and Kanye exited their vehicle across the street from the restaurant and were instantly surrounded by paparazzi. They knew she was coming and surrounded her without impeding her ability to walk into the restaurant. If there are more than a dozen paparazzi, then they were tipped off by the celebrity's publicist. Most nights, there are just a handful of photographers at Craig's waiting to see who arrives.

Another famous location for the stakeout is the *Jimmy Kimmel Live!* rear entrance to the studio. Photographers spend each weekday afternoon standing around waiting for the show's guests to arrive. Show appearances are publicized each day to the media and the show tapes at 5 p.m. Paparazzi typically gather mid-afternoon. Unlike staking out a restaurant, security keeps them about fifty feet away from the rear entrance to the studio; therefore, photographers must rely on their telephoto lenses for detailed images. They are not allowed to approach the celebrity. Instead, the celebrity decides whether or not to walk over to the photographers.

After-parties, as the name implies, occur when an official red carpet event or movie premiere ends. They serve as another venue for a stakeout. For example, after the premiere of *Fast and Furious Presents: Shaw and Hobbs* on Saturday, July 13, 2019, there was an after-party held at Katsuya sushi restaurant on Hollywood Boulevard in Los Angeles. It took place at night, and guests started arriving around 9:30 p.m. The few paparazzi who were there remained outside of the restaurant for the entire party hoping to catch a photo of one of the movie's stars entering or leaving the restaurant. Since the restaurant was rented for this private affair, paparazzi and autograph seekers were placed behind barricades to allow the movie's cast and crew to exit their cars unimpeded. Similar to standing outside a restaurant such as Craig's, the photographers seek the celebrities', directors', and producers' attention by yelling out their names hoping to catch that one photo that can be sold.

THE RED CARPET

The world premiere of *Fast and Furious Presents: Hobbs and Shaw* starring Dwayne Johnson, Jason Statham, and Idris Elba took place on Saturday, July 13, 2019, at the Dolby Theatre on Hollywood Boulevard. At this event, invited guests included the movie's stars, their friends, families, and other actors. Hollywood Boulevard was closed off and a set was built to greet the actors and invited guests including photographers, the type of paparazzi *Entertainment Tonight*'s Kevin Frazier discussed in chapter 2. These photographers stood to the right of the welcome entrance under a pavilion-like structure to take photos of the movie's actors and other celebrities. They remained in position the entire time. Entertainment television programs including *Entertainment Tonight, Access Hollywood,* and *Extra* had small, temporary camera positions in front of the theater's entrance for interviews. The movie's cast arrived in SUV limousines and greeted the crowd lined across the street from the Dolby Theatre.

The premiere's activities began when the cast and crew started arriving one at a time in their limousines. As the movie's cast exits the cars, the crowd yells for them to walk toward them and shake hands, take selfies, and sign autographs. As all this happens, the line of paparazzi photographers in their enclosed area snap photos. They are taking pictures of the movie's cast who are on Hollywood Boulevard interacting with the crowd and those who are posing in front of the movie's posters. The paparazzi cannot leave their designated spot. Similar to the stakeout, these photographers are on their feet for several hours. They arrive and set up starting one to two hours before the premiere starts and leave once it is officially over. Physically, it is a tough job, especially in the summer heat.

These invited paparazzi are more respected by security officials than those who stake out restaurants and the Los Angeles airport. They are invited to the premiere and often work for specific media agencies. Some photographers, such as Vince Flores, used to attend red carpet events or movie premieres *and then* drive around the city looking for more photo opportunities.[8] He earned money working as both types of paparazzi in the same day.

STUDIO CITY FARMERS MARKET AND OTHER OUTDOOR VENUES

Every Sunday the Studio City Farmers Market, located near the major production studios, opens for business. It is also famous for celebrity sightings *and* for the paparazzi who track them. There are not as many photographers as you might see staking out Beverly Hills and Hollywood restaurants, but a dedicated few are there every Sunday walking the one-block open market on Ventura Place. Unlike the stakeout where photographers remain outside a restaurant or other business, these paparazzi walk up and down the market among the crowd of customers.

These paparazzi have walked this street for years. One paparazzo, a regular who visits the farmers market each week, wears a hat that says, "I'm a paparazzi. Deal with it."[9] The head of security for the Studio City Farmers Market, who asked to remain anonymous, said that he sees the same dedicated paparazzi every Sunday. Another paparazzo, who refused to be formally interviewed for this book, said that in his opinion not as many celebrities come to the farmers market as there used to be but enough of them still show up that it's worth him spending time there each Sunday.[10]

Both the security director and photographer said celebrity publicists often contact them to inform them their celebrity client will be at the farmers market on a specific Sunday. This advanced notice of the celebrity's whereabouts is an informal way of promoting themselves in the context of having a "normal" Sunday outing. The paparazzo will take a photo and sell it. The media agency will frame the visit to the farmers market as the celebrity enjoying a day out alone or with family as their new media project is about to launch. And that photo will be published online, in a magazine, or broadcast on television and mention the forthcoming project. The publicist's and celebrity's goals are accomplished. The photographer earns money.

Similar to how mainstream journalism functions, publicists provide the *who, what, when,* and *where* and the paparazzo provides the *how* by taking the photograph. Everyone walks away happy including the paparazzo who gets paid. The farmers market security director noted he often receives calls from TMZ tipping him off that they will be there trailing a specific celebrity.[11] He indicated he does not often see the TMZ field producers. They quietly remain in the background as they record video.

Studio City Farmers Market has a children's play area with a rock-climbing wall, bouncy houses, and a merry-go-round. The security director's challenge is balancing the privacy of families, the right of the paparazzi to walk around, and the overall safety of the vendors, shoppers, and visitors. He indicated that this farmers market is an open, public space for all, including paparazzi. His job is not to restrict access but to protect everyone's safety.

The children's play area is an example of the intended nature and purpose of the California's anti-harassment and privacy laws, Sections 1708.7 and 1708.8 of the civil code.[12] The laws were intended to provide the public, as a whole, with more personal security in their activities. Children, spouses, and partners are all interacting with vendors at this one-block-long farmers market. Section 1708.8 includes language aimed at protecting "familial activity." This includes "interaction with the plaintiff's family or significant others under circumstances in which the plaintiff has a reasonable expectation of privacy."[13] The legal question is whether a celebrity has a reasonable right to privacy *with* their children in the play area. The answer is yes. Children and their parents playing in a physical area with designated activities for them is an example of "intimate" activity and details of their lives under the law.[14] The privacy law does not delineate specific locations beyond private property. Yet, it protects the person who is engaging in a "private, personal, or familial activity," regardless of location.[15]

SEARCHING FOR CELEBRITIES BY CAR

One of the most highly regarded paparazzi in the industry is Giles Harrison. For about twenty years he has driven the streets of Beverly Hills, Hollywood, West Hollywood, and Studio City looking for those celebrities eating at an outdoor café or walking along the sidewalk. His approach is simple: he finds his subjects by driving around the city and taking photos from his SUV. Harrison admits that he spends $200 per week on gas for his Ford Expedition and estimates that he drives about 2,000 miles per month on the streets of Los Angeles.[16] Five days per week, he spends eight to ten hours in his car simply driving and taking photos with his Nikon telephoto lens.[17] Harrison estimates there are about ten paparazzi, including himself, who drive around the city and take photos from their cars.

Harrison's business, London Entertainment, sells both his own photographs and those from freelance photographers he contracts with in Miami, Vancouver, New York City, and of course, Los Angeles. In 2007 during the heyday for paparazzi in Los Angeles, he estimated that he earned

$2,000 per day from the photos he snapped and those from freelance photographers he hired. Now, he earns about $2,000 per week. That amounts to about an 80 percent drop in revenue in recent years. He said he is able to stay working in this business because he invested his money over the years and consolidated his property investments. Harrison knows that the celebrity photography business is suffering now with competition coming from the celebrities themselves who run their own Instagram accounts and often beat the paparazzi by releasing their own exclusives.

Monday, July 15, 2019, was a typical day for Harrison on the job. He drove around the city checking well-known restaurants and coffee shops along Hollywood Boulevard, Melrose Avenue, and other local streets. At a red light on Hollywood Boulevard, a hot pink–colored Corvette turned in front of Harrison's Expedition. That car belonged to longtime local Los Angeles celebrity Angelyne. She became famous beginning in the 1980s when she placed billboards in the city with her provocative image and telephone number written on them.[18] Upon seeing her Corvette, Harrison immediately made a U-turn and followed her to a Starbucks located on Argyle Avenue and Sunset Boulevard.

The sixty-one-year-old model and actress stood on Sunset Boulevard posing for photographs and selling her memorabilia. Harrison quickly grabbed his camera and took a few dozen photos. At first, he was not able to snap a photo of Angelyne by herself. When she entered the Starbucks, Harrison moved his car and parked behind the pink Corvette. He waited thirty minutes. When Angelyne exited Starbucks and walked back to her car, Harrison quickly snapped the full-length photo he wanted.

Harrison explained that his many photos of Angelyne serve several purposes. The first is to have several photos taken from different angles to choose from to send to his agent. Secondly, he wanted to increase his archive of photos. As a sixty-one-year-old personality, he knows the day will come when she may fade from the public eye in Los Angeles and retire and he may be able to supply a requested photo from his archives. From this one encounter outside the Starbucks, he believed he ccould produce four story narratives from these photos: Angelyne's fashion, selling her collectables from the trunk of her car, the visual of the pink Corvette she drives, and combining the first three into one large story.

At the end of the workday, Harrison sent his photos of Angelyne to his agent. In return the agent sold them to websites, newspapers, and magazines earning a 30 percent commission. Harrison kept the other 70 percent for himself. After taking the photos of Angelyne, Harrison turned on his car and started looking for his next photo opportunity.

NOTES

1. The author respects the requests for identities to remain anonymous.
2. The security specialist, who wishes to remain anonymous, works several red carpet and movie premiere events per year. Interview held on Saturday, July 13, 2019.
3. Ibid.
4. Many interviews yielded an estimate of forty to one hundred total paparazzi. Photographers disagree on the estimated number but they unanimously agree it could not be more than one hundred full- and part-time photographers.
5. Ibid.
6. Interview with a former TMZ field producer, Friday, July 12, 2019.
7. Ibid.
8. Interview with Vince Flores, Tuesday, July 16, 2019.
9. Ibid.
10. Sunday, July 14, 2019. Second anonymous paparazzo.
11. Sunday, July 14, 2019. Interview with the director of security at the Studio City Farmers Market. He wished to remain anonymous.
12. Cal. Civ. Code §1708.7 (2018) and Cal. Civ. Code §1708.8 (2018).
13. Cal. Civ. Code §1708.8 (7)(1)(l)(B) (2018).
14. Cal. Civ. Code §1708.8 (7)(1)(l)(A) (2018).
15. Cal. Civ. Code §1708.8 (b) (2018).
16. Interview and observation of Giles Harrison on Monday, July 15, 2019.
17. Ibid.
18. According to the IMDb website, Angleyne has appeared in several movies including *Earth Girls Are Easy, The Malibu Beach Vampires,* and *Dangerous Love.*

SIX

The Constitutional Dangers in Censoring Paparazzi

"These people [i.e., the printers] think they have a right to everything, however secret or sacred."

—Thomas Jefferson (1815)

The First Amendment promises freedom of the press from government oversight. Despite Thomas Jefferson's thoughts about how the printers and publishers of his time were entitled to private information, he was, nonetheless, an advocate for press freedoms. In 1799, he told his friend Elbridge Gerry the important role of the press in society, "I am . . . for freedom of the press and against all violation of the Constitution to silence by force and not by reason the complaints or criticism, just or unjust, of our citizens against the conduct of their agents."[1] The Constitution's First Amendment guarantees that government does not interfere with the right to publish. That guarantee exists at both the federal and state levels of government and society.[2]

States, including California, cannot pass laws that limit or punish the media's freedom without a strong, legal foundation. The media's freedom includes the rights of the paparazzi to do their jobs. The Supreme Court has a broad history of providing the press with freedom to publish unless it is a rare instance of a national security issue. Legal censorship is often referred to as content-based limits on publishing.[3] This can include writings that are libelous, threatening, obscene, or contain false advertising.[4] The part of California's privacy law that imposes a financial penalty is a form of censorship.[5] American media rights include prohibiting governments at the federal, state, or local levels from imposing financial penalties for published content.

This chapter provides a concluding critique of the constitutional weaknesses in California's privacy and anti-harassment laws discussed in this book as they apply to the paparazzi media. It provides alternative ways the state can protect celebrities (and the public) from privacy intrusions and harassment without imposing unnecessary First Amendment freedom of the press obstacles on paparazzi and media companies who publish or broadcast paparazzi photos and videos.

SUPREME COURT DECISIONS PROTECT MEDIA RIGHTS

Simply put, in the United States the media have constitutionally broad rights to publish and broadcast information including content that may be deemed controversial. The Supreme Court decisions discussed in this section reflect the vast, constitutionally protected legal freedoms of the media. One of the most important decisions in the twentieth century that upheld this fundamental right was the 1964 *Times v. Sullivan* ruling by the Supreme Court.[6] In a 9-0 ruling, the Court unanimously held that public figures must prove actual malice if they believe their reputations have been harmed by the press. Actual malice means an intent to harm, knowing the published information is false. The Court stated this actual malice standard was needed because public officials (politicians and other public leaders) legitimately open themselves up to criticism in the performance of their public jobs. The decisions they make may be controversial, and they should expect tough criticism. The *Times v. Sullivan* decision focused entirely on political and government leaders, but the Court in later years expanded public officials to include others. In *Gertz v. Welch* in 1974, the Court defined who public figures are to include those who live their lives full-time or partially (temporarily) in the public eye.[7] In this decision, Justice Lewis Powell provided an important perspective on how public figures (such as celebrities) can use the media to their advantage when they believed they are wronged:

> The first remedy of any victim of defamation is self-help—using available opportunities to contradict the lie or correct the error, and thereby to minimize its adverse impact on reputation. Public officials and public figures usually enjoy significantly greater access to the channels of effective communication, and hence have a more realistic opportunity to counteract false statements than private individuals normally enjoy.[8]

It can be argued that Hollywood's actors, directors, producers, and writers who live in the public eye often do so intentionally to promote their careers. They are likened to what Justice Powell called voluntary public figures:

> Some occupy positions of such persuasive power and influence that they are deemed public figures for all purposes. More commonly, those classed as public figures have thrust themselves to the forefront of particular public controversies in order to influence the resolution of the issues involved. In either event, they invite attention and comment.[9]

Essentially, those who work in Hollywood and are known publicly open themselves up for the attention they are nonetheless seeking. That attention often comes from paparazzi. It is important to remember that Justice Powell's words reflect a reality. Celebrities have wide access to the media not just to promote their careers but to defend themselves if they believe their privacy has been invaded or their reputations harmed by the paparazzi.

While decisions such as *Times v. Sullivan* and *Gertz v. Welch* established a legal standard by which we can categorize celebrities, we can look to other Supreme Court decisions that provide a guide for the legal rights of the press and media more broadly. In 1974's *Miami Herald Publishing Company v. Tornillo,* the Supreme Court ruled unanimously that a newspaper cannot be told where, when, or how to publish a political reply to a newspaper's editorial criticism. One of the Court's most important statements in the decision is that "press responsibility is not mandated by the Constitution, and like many other virtues it cannot be legislated."[10] This decision provided strong support for a publication's own editorial decisions. This ruling provides clarity of the dubious nature of California's privacy law related to sanctioning the press for publishing photos of celebrities without their permission.[11] The Supreme Court in *Tornillo* explicitly backed the First Amendment rights of publishers: "A responsible press is an undoubtedly desirable goal, but press responsibility is not mandated by the Constitution, and, like many other virtues, *it cannot be legislated*."[12] Beyond this important decision, the Supreme Court has historically looked down upon any attempt to restrict the print media's editorial freedoms.[13]

Another Supreme Court ruling that more closely parallels controversial paparazzi behavior in California is the 1988 *Hustler v. Falwell* decision.[14] *Hustler* magazine, a pornographic publication, published a satirical Campari Liquor advertisement in 1983 with former Christian pastor and televangelist Jerry Falwell alleging in an "interview" that his first sexual experience was with his mother in an outhouse. This interview never actually took place since this was a fictional "advertisement" for Campari liquor. Campari had a tradition of publishing advertisements with famous customers. *Hustler* published this satirical advertisement as a means of mocking Falwell. Falwell and *Hustler* publisher, Larry Flynt, were publicly sparring over the legitimacy of pornography in American society.

Jerry Falwell sued *Hustler* and Larry Flynt, alleging invasion of privacy and intentional infliction of emotional distress. In a unanimous decision, the Supreme Court ruled on behalf of *Hustler*. It said that the advertisement was satirical and not to be taken seriously since in two sections of the magazine it was labeled both as parody and fictional. Since Falwell was a public figure when he was alive and led a crusade against pornography, he opened himself up to public criticism. This advertisement, though not tasteful, was a legitimate form of criticism by Hustler, according to the Supreme Court.

While the *Hustler* decision by the Supreme Court focused on the intentional infliction of emotional distress accusation by Falwell, it serves as another legal precedent for why the part of California's anti-paparazzi law, Section 1708.8 that is focused on punishing the media, may be unconstitutional. Paparazzi take photos and videos of celebrities. Just as Falwell was a public figure and invited attention to his actions, so do celebrities. It is very difficult to prove invasion of privacy and intentional infliction of emotional of distress when your day-to-day activities are public. In *Hustler v. Falwell*, the Supreme Court set a high standard for public figures to recover any damages based on an allegation of intentional infliction of emotional distress:

> We conclude that public figures and public officials may not recover for the tort of intentional infliction of emotional distress by reason of publications such as the one here at issue without showing, in addition, that the publication contains a false statement of fact which was made with "actual malice," i.e., with knowledge that the statement was false or with reckless disregard as to whether or not it was true.[15]

In order for any celebrity to successfully sue a paparazzo for intentional emotional damage, actual malice will need to be shown by the victim. Proving actual malice or outright intentional of harm toward the celebrity is difficult. A California or federal district court would remind the plaintiff they live their life openly as a public personality. There would need to be some type of visual evidence proving any paparazzo acted with intent to act.

A 1972 Supreme Court decision provides even more clarity on why Section 1708.8 of the Civil Code may be an unconstitutional restriction on press freedoms. In *Branzburg v. Hayes*, Chief Justice Byron White wrote in the opinion that the press in the United States have a wide range of freedoms.[16] In this specific case, the Supreme Court had to decide if the First Amendment's press freedoms included the right to protect a confidential source if a reporter is asked to disclose that identity to a grand jury. In writing the decision, Chief Justice White laid out the overall press freedoms in the United States within the context of the *Branzburg* case:

> . . . without some protection for seeking out the news, freedom of the press could be eviscerated. But these cases involve no intrusions upon

> speech or assembly, no prior restraint or restriction on what the press may publish, and no express or implied command that the press publish what it prefers to withhold. No exaction or tax for the privilege of publishing, and no penalty, civil or criminal, related to the content of published material is at issue here.[17]

What the Chief Justice stated is that there is no controversy about American press freedoms. There is little to no government-sponsored censorship, taxation, or other criminal penalties applied to the media.

California's law that imposes a penalty on media who publish celebrity photos without permission and as an act of invasion of privacy is a restriction on the press's rights.[18] It states: "If the plaintiff proves that the invasion of privacy was committed for a commercial purpose, the person shall also be subject . . . to a civil fine of not less than five thousand dollars ($5,000) and not more than fifty thousand dollars ($50,000)."[19] Commercial purpose means selling the photos for sale or other financial gain.[20] It is also defined as proof of sale, publication, or transmission of content.[21] Beyond the paparazzi, the law applies to "a person who directs, solicits, actually induces, or actually causes another person, regardless of whether there is an employer-employee relationship."[22] These are the people whom paparazzi often contract their services with or work for in a full-time capacity. Essentially, both the paparazzi and the media companies they work for may be subject to this law if either party knew there was an act of invasion of privacy. The legal problem beyond the financial penalties aspect of the law is proving that photographers and media companies *knowingly* invaded privacy. A likely defense is that either or both parties can easily deny any knowledge of any privacy violations. In 2001 in *Bartnicki v. Vopper*, the Supreme Court decided a case where a radio host received illegally intercepted and recorded audio and played it on air.[23] In that decision, the Court ruled the radio host had a right to broadcast the audio since he did not know it was illegally recorded. Any media company using paparazzi-generated images or videos can claim the same defense.

The First Amendment allows broadcasters to air materials it receives even if they are illegally gathered. This raises the question of whether Section 1808.8's provision violates the First Amendment rights of publishers who receive photos or videos of celebrities even if they are obtained illegally. In this scenario, the legal burden is on the paparazzo who produced the content, *not* the website, television show, or magazine that publishes it.[24]

Section 1708.7 of the California's Civil Code, the anti-paparazzi harassment law, also has serious freedom of the press consequences. It is a crime to stalk someone as they go about their daily activities.[25] It is a fine line between stalking and tracking someone. Yet, paparazzi often track and monitor their celebrity subjects as they move about in public areas.

The law exempts reporters in the context of newsgathering "conduct" connected to a newsworthy event.[26] But even this exemption in the law is not as clear as it should be. What constitutes a newsworthy event within the entertainment world? A red carpet event? Outdoor filming of a movie? A movie premiere? Meeting an agent or attorney at an outdoor restaurant? In those circumstances it is the job of paparazzi to take photos. In the daily public activities of celebrities, what constitutes a newsworthy event is relative. In the pursuit of celebrity news, paparazzi (often working in teams of photographers) follow their celebrity subjects. If the celebrity is in an open and public setting, then paparazzi have the right to take photographs.

The law makes it a crime to "annoy" or "harass" someone, in this case presumably celebrities.[27] From the celebrity's perspective "annoy" and "harass" can apply to paparazzi even in the course of their work. The paparazzi media do not consider their work as harassment but legitimate reporting. Any celebrity who is distressed by seeing paparazzi at a Starbucks, the Los Angeles airport, or walking on Rodeo Drive might consider themselves harassed and annoyed under the law. That's not fair to the photographers who are in public areas doing their jobs and have a right to be there.

FAMOUS (OR INFAMOUS) PAPARAZZO RON GALELLA

While California's anti-harassment and invasion of privacy laws may violate the First Amendment's freedom of the press guarantees, this does not mean that paparazzi are entitled to act in malicious ways toward their celebrity subjects. Celebrities are entitled to privacy in their homes with their families. They should expect some privacy with their families even in public areas and should not be threatened or made to feel that they or their families' lives are in danger. There is no free speech or press protection for legitimate threats made against anyone. One need only look back in history to the constant surveillance conducted on Princess Diana in the years leading up to her death, including the infamous car chase involving the paparazzi.

Famous paparazzo Ron Galella unyieldingly pursued photos of Jackie Onassis (President John F. Kennedy's wife) in the 1970s and 1980s. He relentlessly followed her and her children in New York City. He stood outside their home and their schools, and seemed to be ever-present wherever they traveled in the city. Galella physically imposed himself on the family and restricted their movements in order to take a photo. Clearly, he went too far in his actions. According to court records, at one point he jumped out of the bushes to take a photo while Onassis's son, John Kennedy Jr., was riding his bicycle, causing him to swerve his bike and nearly crash.[28] He also interfered with Onassis's daughter, Caroline Kennedy's tennis lessons. Galella had a record of trailing the family by car or boat and even bribed local restaurant and business owners for inside information.[29] His actions not only interfered with the family's privacy, but also their daily activities. It caused the Secret Service to intervene on their behalf on multiple occasions.

In 1973 the federal circuit court in New York granted a physical injunction to keep Galella a specific distance away from the family. He was enjoined from "harassing, alarming, startling, tormenting, touching the person of the defendant . . . or her children . . . and from blocking their movements in the public places and thoroughfares, invading their immediate zone of privacy by means of physical movements, gestures or with photographic equipment and from performing any act reasonably calculated to place the lives and safety of the defendant . . . and her children in jeopardy."[30] Galella had clearly violated any sense of privacy Onassis and her family deserved. A federal court ordered him to stay one hundred feet away from both children and fifty yards away from Onassis at all times.[31] Additionally, Galella could only contact the family through their attorney, and he could not use their names, photo, or portraits for promoting any of his professional photography projects.[32]

In the first trial between Galella and Onasis, the federal district court found there was overwhelming evidence he was guilty of harassment, intentional infliction of emotional distress, assault, and battery, invasion of privacy, and profiting off of Onassis and her children through commercial exploitation of their images.[33] All these criminal acts occurred in his dogged and endless quest for family photos. While Galella's actions were extreme, it nonetheless serves as an important lesson for any paparazzo today who may go too far in a hunt for photos and videos.

While the federal court found Galella guilty of interfering in the affairs of Onassis's family, it did agree that Onassis, as a public figure, was a legitimate news story. As a "newsman," Galella's actions went beyond what was considered reasonable in covering her family for news.[34] While the First Amendment protects the press's right to report on the activities of noteworthy public figures, the court noted it is not a "a wall of immunity protecting newsmen from any liability for their conduct while gathering news. There is no such scope to the First Amendment right."[35] Plainly, the paparazzi are not above the law. They cannot put others' lives in danger or physically interfere with the daily life of their subjects.

The actions by Galella in the 1970s and 1980s against Onassis and her children offer an important lesson for any of today's paparazzi. It is legitimate and legal to stand outside a restaurant, business, or airport waiting for a celebrity but another thing to physically impose yourself on a celebrity subject. The California anti-harassment and privacy laws clearly try to protect the physical and emotional well-being of celebrities.[36] It is not and should not be legal to threaten someone or harass them to the point they cannot live a normal life. Celebrities and their families should feel secure in their homes and at other personal properties. They should be able to enjoy solitude with their families. This is the very complaint that Prince Harry and Meghan Markle have toward paparazzi who are attempting to take photos of their son, Archie.

PROTECTING MEDIA RIGHTS IN CALIFORNIA

On first read, both Sections 1708.7 and 1708.8 of California's Civil Code are good faith efforts to reduce overt privacy intrusions and harassment activities aimed at celebrities. Even though celebrities, as a group, are not formally written into the law and it applies to all Californians, it is well known they are the targeted population at risk. The anti-harassment and stalking law, Section 1708.7, is wide ranging and covers criminal activities concerning credible threats that lead to substantial emotional distress. This includes the use of electronics and repeated verbal and physical means to scare a victim.

As discussed in this book, there are many areas of the laws that are ripe for constitutional review by federal or state courts. At some point, there could very well be a lawsuit by a media organization or freelance paparazzo that addresses the negative impact a section or several provisions of 1708.7 or 1708.8 have on their free press rights. While one can never predict when a court challenge will be convened, California legislators can take the initiative sooner rather than later to narrow the focus of the laws and create media exceptions to these laws while at the same time protecting celebrities' privacy and safety.

Despite Section 1708.7 providing an exception for a "newsworthy event," there is no written acknowledgment in the law of the newsworthy, noteworthy, and public lives of certain individuals who reside in California. This is a major gap in the law that could impact the legitimate freedom of press for paparazzi. Fundamentally, any entertainment reporter or paparazzo would argue that their celebrity beat is newsworthy and often filled with events or activities the public should know about. Their job is to be where the celebrities are at those occasions.

As explained in chapter 3, whether we like it or not, paparazzi do their jobs by following celebrities who are out in public; therefore, they *monitor* and *surveil* their movements in what could be interpreted as a violation of Section 1708.7.[37] It is not harassment unless a photographer overtly threatens or acts as a constant physical nuisance, as Ron Galella acted toward Onassis and her family. The wording of the law needs to explicitly exempt media who work on newsworthy stories, not just a specific "newsworthy event."[38] Anything less than a specific reference to media or press in the law continues to put paparazzi at risk.

State leaders can easily amend Section 1708.7 to provide more protection for the legitimate functions of the media, including paparazzi. The subsection of the law that states: "For purposes of the liability created by subdivision (a), 'place under surveillance' also does not include any newsgathering conduct connected to a newsworthy event."[39] Another one or two sentences that clarifies "conduct" would simply state that newsgathering includes following and monitoring those individuals who are a part of a news story or event. A clarification of "conduct" would exempt photographers from harassment and put the focus of the law where it should be: on those criminals who genuinely stalk and harass victims with potential physical harm.

There is also a straightforward approach to amend Section 1708.8, the invasion of privacy law. On first read it is an important means of protecting celebrities and their families' privacy. Clearly, they are entitled to lead private lives to a substantial degree. While this is a well-meaning cause, the part of the law focused on punishing the media (paparazzi, photo agencies, and others) for knowingly purchasing, publishing, or transmitting photos or videos recorded in violation of someone's privacy is overbroad and punitive toward the press and violates their media rights. As discussed in this chapter, there are too many phrases in Section 1708.8 that negatively impact the paparazzi industry's freedom of press. The press cannot be directly or indirectly censored or otherwise penalized without showing a direct harm to society. The penalties within the law amount to an informal form of prior restraint and censorship, and in this circumstance, it is unconstitutional.

Rather than focus on the "commercial" aspect of the law and who purchased and sold media content, the California State Assembly should focus its legislative efforts on whether the specific media content in question violates someone's privacy. It can establish a legal standard that emphasizes how the material in question invaded privacy or even harmed someone's reputation. Media attorney Mickey Osterreicher is correct when he advocates that the privacy law should incorporate language from the state's shield law that describes who is recognized as a journalist within the context of protecting confidential sources.[40] Formally recognizing the wide variety of media occupations within the privacy law eliminates the need for tracking down who sold content to what company. Put the focus on the questionable media content itself. This will avoid the unnecessary threats of financial fines on the media. Essentially, from a journalist perspective, focus on the *what* (the questionable content) first. The *who* (offending party) will naturally be determined later.

One means of protecting the rights of photographers is to legally guarantee that paparazzi can work, but the public, including celebrities, have "safety zones" so their movements are not impeded in any way, as attorney Tara Sattler suggested in chapter 3.[41] Her approach is content neutral and focuses on the physical safety of the public. It does not impede on paparazzi. The California Assembly could determine a physical boundary that photographers would be prohibited from breaching. This assures the public a physical zone of privacy. The federal courts imposed safety zones on Ron Galella when he overstepped his boundaries with Jackie Onassis's family.

Where California elected officials have not placed a burden on media rights is in the state's vehicle code discussed in chapter 3. In order to protect *all* motorists, no one, including paparazzi, can chase after someone in their car and take photos while driving the car. This time, place, and manner approach does not impact journalism practices in any way. Rather, Section 40008 of the California Vehicle Code is about the physical safety of all motorists.[42] The impact of the law on paparazzi is secondary to the priority of motorists driving safely. That same approach can be applied to paparazzi who walk the streets of Beverly Hills or stand outside restaurants looking for subjects. The safety of the public should always be a priority without impacting photographers' press rights.

FINAL PERSPECTIVES ON PAPARAZZI

Within reasonable privacy arguments, as public figures celebrities are going to be the subject of public attention, not just at galas and premieres. Just as they should expect that strangers will ask for selfies and autographs, celebrities should expect to have their photos taken by fans and the paparazzi. This is a just consequence to leading a public life.

The days of the individual paparazzo climbing a fence or stealing someone's trash are over. It rarely, if ever, occurs. If and when that happens, there is no debate that a photographer should be prosecuted for invasion of privacy. Love or hate the paparazzi, they fill the public's demand for celebrity photos. Within that demand, those who work as paparazzi are entitled to the promise of press freedoms in the United States. California cannot interfere with that unless the government has a specific reason to issue a content-based restriction. Those press restrictions apply in circumstances of real, imminent threats, not simply for calls to safeguard privacy.

In chapter 1, actress Jennifer Aniston was quoted as saying, "I'm fed up with the sport-like scrutiny and body shaming that occurs daily under the guise of 'journalism,' the 'First Amendment' and 'celebrity news.'"[43] She vehemently disagreed with the idea that the First Amendment recognized the works of tabloid photographers and writers. While her frustrations with paparazzi are understandable and we can empathize with her, she and others who remain in the public spotlight need to come to terms with the fact that celebrity photographers would not follow her if she was not highly sought after as a commercial commodity or brand. Unfortunately, sacrificing some areas of privacy comes with her choice of career. If she wants to live a private life, she can easily relocate beyond metropolitan Los Angeles, where she knows her stature as a hot commodity for celebrity-focused magazines and websites will decrease.

Aniston attempts to control her image through social media with an Instagram account and shares career or personal news as she desires and therefore bypasses a lot of the paparazzi demand for her image. For her fifty-first birthday on February 11, 2020, she posted twenty-five times to her Instagram account of nearly thirty million viewers. That is a strong example of Aniston actively controlling her own message. As long as paparazzi act within the bounds of California's privacy and anti-harassment laws, then celebrities such as Aniston must simply recognize the paparazzi reflect the public's interest in her professional and personal life. That may also include photographers circling her house looking for shots.

The Jennifer Anistons of Hollywood can look to the Supreme Court's commentary in *Gertz v. Welch* about the role they play within the celebrity-media bubble: "Public officials and public figures usually enjoy significantly greater access to the channels of effective communication, and hence have a more realistic opportunity to counteract false statements than private individuals normally enjoy."[44] Many celebrities actively use their own media channels such as Instagram or Snapchat to give the public the narrative they choose for themselves. The paparazzi know this often takes away the power of becoming the first to tell the public the story and therefore the value of their photos decrease. Publishing an article in the *Huffington Post* is a direct example of Aniston's media empowerment. Kristen Bell's Twitter campaign is another example of strong use of the media to advocate for change.

Halle Berry or Jennifer Garner may be looking to the California government or another authority to impose a form of legal morality within the media, but that is unlikely to happen. Celebrities need only look no further than the Supreme Court's 1974 *Tornillo* decision about press and morality when the Court stated: "Press responsibility is not mandated by the Constitution, and, like many other virtues, it cannot be legislated."[45] In the United States, a free press is about the right to record and produce photos and videos about those individuals who live their lives in front of the public. A free press includes paparazzi.

NOTES

1. Thomas Jefferson wrote a letter to Elbridge Gerry dated January 26, 1799.
2. The 14th Amendment to the Constitution states that "No State shall make or enforce any law which shall abridge the privileges or immunities of citizens of the United States; nor shall any State deprive any person of life, liberty, or property, without the due process of law; nor deny to any person within its jurisdiction the equal protection of the law." The Supreme Court has interpreted the 14th Amendment as applying to the states. No state can deny its citizens rights provided for in the Constitution.

3. *United States v. Progressive, Inc.* 467 F. Supp 990 (1979). In this case a federal district court censored publication of restricted data contained in the article: "The H-Bomb Secret: How We Got It, Why We're Telling It."

4. See *New York Times v. Sullivan*, 376 U.S. 254 (1964), *Miller v. California*, 413 U.S.15 (1973), and *Central Hudson Gas and Electric Corp. v. Public Service Commission of New York*, 447 U.S. 557 (1980). Each of these Supreme Court decisions established foundations for the limits of the First Amendment in particular speech and publication areas. The Court's decisions in these cases are often referred to by its own decisions in similar matters or by lower federal and state courts.

5. California's privacy law, §1708.8 of the Civil Code, imposes a financial penalty on anyone, including media companies, who publishes or broadcasts information that a victim believes invaded their privacy.

6. 376 U.S. 254 (1964).

7. 418 U.S. 323 (1974).

8. Ibid., 344.

9. Ibid., 345.

10. *Miami Herald Publishing Company v. Tornillo*, 418 U.S. 241, 256 (1974).

11. Cal. Civ. Code §1708.8 (d)-(f) (2018)

12. *Miami Herald Publishing Co.* at 256. Author's italicization.

13. See *Associated Press v. United States*, 326 U.S.1 (1945), *Columbia Broadcasting System, Inc. v. Democratic National Committee*, 412 U.S. 94 (1973), and *Pittsburgh Press Co. v. Human Relations Commission*, 413 U.S. 376 (1973). In all three cases, the Supreme Court supported the rights of the press to make editorial decisions on content.

14. *Hustler Magazine Inc. v. Falwell*, 485 U.S. 46 (1988)

15. Ibid., 56.

16. 408 U.S. 665 (1972)

17. Ibid., 681.

18. Cal. Civ. Code §1708.8 (d)-(f) (2018).

19. Ibid.

20. Cal. Civ. Code §1708.8 (k) (2018).

21. Ibid.

22. Cal. Civ. Code §1808.8 (e) (2018).

23. 532 U.S. 514 (2001).

24. See *Smith v. Daily Mail Publishing Co.*, 443 U.S 97 (1979), and *Florida Star v. BJF*, 491 U.S. 524 (1989). In *Smith v. Daily Mail Publishing Co.* the Supreme Court ruled that while a minor's identity was illegally obtained, the newspaper was entitled to publish the identity within the context of the story. In *Florida Star v. BJF*, the Supreme Court stated a newspaper did not violate a sexual assault victim's identity since that information was publicly available.

25. Cal. Civ. Code §1708.7 (B)(b)4 (2018).

26. Ibid.

27. Cal. Civ. Code §1708.7 (B)(b)5 (2018). "Harass" means a knowing and willful course of conduct directed at a specific person which seriously alarms, annoys, torments, or terrorizes the person, and which serves no legitimate purpose. The course of conduct must be such as would cause a reasonable person to suffer substantial emotional distress, and must actually cause substantial emotional distress to the person.

28. *Gallela v. Onassis*, 487 F. 2d 986 (1973).

29. Ibid., 992.

30. Ibid.

31. Ibid., 993.

32. Ibid.

33. Ibid., 994.

34. Ibid., 995.

35. Ibid.

36. Cal. Civ. Code §1708.7 (2018) and Cal. Civ. Code §1708.8 (2018).

37. Cal. Civ. Code §1708.7 (3)(B)(2) (2018).

38. Cal. Civ. Code §1708.7 (3)(B)(4) (2018).
39. Cal. Civ. Code §1708.7 (3)(B)(b)(6)(2018).
40. Cal. Const. Art. 1 §2(b).
41. Tara Sattler, "Comment, Plagued by the Paparazzi: How California Should Sharpen the Focus on Its Not-So-Picture-Perfect Paparazzi Laws," *Southwest Law Review*, no. 40 (2010): 43.
42. Cal. Veh. Code §40008 (2018).
43. Jennifer Aniston, "For the Record," *Huffington Post*, July 12, 2016.
44. 418 U.S. 323, 344 (1974).
45. *Miami Herald Publishing Company v. Tornillo*, 418 U.S. 241, 256 (1974).

Bibliography

Aniston, Jennifer. "For the Record," *Huffington Post*, July 12, 2016.

Associated Press v. United States, 326 U.S.1 (1945).

Bartnicki v. Vopper, 532 U.S. 514 (2001).

Boorstin, Daniel. *The Image: A Guide to Pseudo-Events in America* (New York: Vintage 1961).

Branzburg v. Hayes, 408 U.S. 665 (1972).

Buhl, Jennifer. (Freelance photographer) in discussion with author, April 2018.

Burns, Bridgett. "13 Celebrities on Protecting Their Privacy," *Marie Claire*, August 2, 2017, https://www.marieclaire.com/celebrity/news/g4914/celebrities-privacy-quotes/.

Burnett, David. (Freelance photojournalist) in discussion with author, January 2018.

Cal. Civ. Code §1708.7 (2014).

Cal. Civ. Code §1708.8 (2014).

Cal. Civ. Code §1708.7 (2018).

Cal. Civ. Code §1708.8 (2018).

Cal. Const. Art. 1 §2(b).

Cal. Penal Code § 11414 (2014).

Cal. Veh. Code §40008 (2015).

Cal. Veh. Code §40008 (2018).

"Celebrity," an episode in *Morgan Spurlock, Inside Man.*

Central Hudson Gas and Electric Corp. v. Public Service Commission of New York, 447 U.S. 557 (1980).

Choi, Chong Ju and Berger, Ron. "Ethics of Celebrities and Their Increasing Influence in 21st Century Society," *Journal of Business Ethics*, Vol. 91 (2010).

Chéroux, Clément. "Thirteen and a Half Theories on the Concept of Paparazzi Photography," *Paparazzi! Photographers, Stars, Artists*, ed. Clément Chéroux (France: Flammarion, 2014).

Chéroux, Clémont, Lenglois, Camille, Léon, Véra, and Bonhomme, Max. "Hazards of the Trade: Interviews with Paparazzi," in *Paparazzi! Photographers, Stars, Artists* ed. Clément Chéroux (Paris: Flammarion, 2014).

Cohen, Belinda. [psued.] (Former editor, *People* magazine) in discussion with author, March 2018.

Columbia Broadcasting System, Inc. v. Democratic National Committee, 412 U.S. 94 (1973).

Cook, Christopher. "The Making of Modern Celebrity: Famous for Fifteen Minutes—and Longer" (presentation, Gresham College Lecture, London, UK, Wednesday, February 9, 2011).

Danly, Cameron. "Paparazzi and the Search for Federal Legislation," *Washington State University Law Review*, no. 38 (2011).

Daunt, Tina. "Jennifer Garner Joins Halle Berry in Fight for Tougher Anti-Parazzi Law," *The Hollywood Reporter*, August 14, 2013, http://www.hollywoodreporter.com/news/jennifer-garner-joins-halle-berry-60641.

Downes, Lawrence. "Looks Like the Steven Tyler Act Is Sunk," *New York Times*, March 21, 2013. http://takingnote.blogs.nytimes.com/2013/03/21/looks-like-the-steven-tyler-act-is-sunk/.

Dube, Rebecca. "The amazing way Kristen Bell confronted paparazzi taking photos of her children," May 6, 2018, https://www.today.com/parents/kristen-bell-confronted-paparazzi-photographing-her-children-t128440.

D'Zurillo, Christie. (Entertainment reporter, *Los Angeles Times*) in discussion with author, February 2018.

Federal Aviation Authority UAS Symposium, Local and State UAS Enforcement Authorities, March 27, 2017, https://www.faa.gov/uas/resources/events_calendar/archive/2017_uas_symposium/media/Workshop_7_Local_and_State_UAS_Enforcement_Authorities.pdf.

Flores, Vince. (Photographer) in discussion with author, July 2019.

Florida Star v. BJF, 491 U.S. 524 (1989).

Frazier, Kevin. (Co-host, *Entertainment Tonight*) in discussion with author, February 2018.

Galella v. Onassis, 487 F.2d 986 (2d Cir. 1973).

Gajda, Amy. *The First Amendment Bubble: How Privacy and Paparazzi Threaten a Free Press* (Cambridge, Massachusetts: Harvard University Press, 2015).

Gardner, Eriq. "California Law Punishing Paparazzi for High-Speed Celebrity Chases Is Upheld," *The Hollywood Reporter*, September 30, 2015, http://www.hollywoodreporter.com/thr-esq/california-law-punishing-paparazzi-high-828437.

Gertz v. Welch, 418 U.S. 323 (1974).

Gross, Michael Joseph. "Michael Jackson's Last Close-Up," *Vanity Fair*, June 1, 2009.

Haidrani, Salma. "Charitable Celebrities: The Stars Who Give Back," *Glamour*, October 4, 2017, http://www.glamourmagazine.co.uk/gallery/charitable-celebrities-stars-who-do-good.

"Halle Berry happy about anti-Paparazzi bill passage," *USA Today*, September 25, 2013, https://www.usatoday.com/story/life/people/2013/09/25/california-gov-jerry-brown-signs-anti-paparazzi-bill/2870965/.

Harrison, Giles. (Owner, London Entertainment Group and paparazzo) in discussion with author, April 2018.

Hill v. Thomas, 973 P.2d 1246, 1255 (Colo. 1999).

HRS § 711-1110.9 (2016).

HRS § 711-1111(1)(e) (2016).

Interview with paparazzo Giles Harrison, July 15, 2019.

Interview with 50 Cent, June 17, 2019.

Jacquet, Dale. *Journalistic Ethics: Moral Responsibility in the Media* (Upper Saddle River, New Jersey: Pearson 2007).

Jerslev, Anne and Mortensen, Mette. "Taking the extra out of the extraordinary: Paparazzi photography as celebrity news genre on the Internet," *International Journal of Cultural Studies*, 17(6).

Kagan, Elaine. "Confessions of a Paparazzo," *Los Angeles Magazine*, February 25, 2015, http://www.lamag.com/longform/confessions-paparazzo/.

Kelogg, Sam. [psued] (Getty, 20th Century FOX, and Instar Images freelance photographer) in discussion with author, February 2018.

Kissell, Rick. "3-Day Ratings: 'Survivor,' 'Keeping Up With the Kardashians' Still Going Strong," *Variety*, May 6, 2016, http://variety.com/2016/tv/news/3-day-ratings-survivor-keeping-up-with-the-kardashians-1201768322/.

"Kristen Bell and Dax Shepard lead campaign to protect kids from paparazzi," *CBSnews.com*, February 28, 2014, https://www.cbsnews.com/news/kristen-bell-and-dax-shepard-start-campagin-to-protect-children-from-paparazzi/.

Lady Gaga, *Paparazzi*. Interscope Records. Originally released July 6, 2009.

Lam, Katherine. "Scarlett Johansson Taken to Los Angeles Police Station Following Paparazzi Incident," FOXNews.com, April 9, 2019, https://www.foxnews.com/entertainment/scarlett-johansson-taken-to-los-angeles-police-station-following-paparazzi-incident.

Lee, Matthew. "Strict Liability and the Anti-Paparazzi Act: The Best Solution to Protect Children of Celebrities," *Hastings Law Journal*, Vol. 66 (2015).

Locke, Christina M. "Does Anti-Paparazzi Mean Anti-Press? First Amendment Implications of Privacy Legislation for the Newsroom," *Seton Hall Journal of Sports & Entertainment Law*, no. 20 (2010).

LoMonte, Frank. (Director, Brechner Center for Freedom of Information) in discussion with author, January 2018.

Marchese, David. "Wendy Williams Wants to Be the Realest in the Game," *The New York Times Magazine*, August 26, 2019, https://www.nytimes.com/interactive/2019/08/26/magazine/wendy-williams-interview.html?smid=nytcore-ios-share.

McNamara, Kim. *Paparazzi: Media Practices and Celebrity Culture* (Malden, MA: Polity 2016).

Miami Herald Publishing Company v. Tornillo, 418 U.S. 241, 256 (1974).

Miller v. California, 413 U.S.15 (1973).

Milne, Carly. "Kristen Bell on the Paparazzi Stalking Children: 'I Saw a Problem, Attacked It Like a Mother, and Actually Made a Difference,'" *Yahoo! Entertainment*, May 6, 2016, https://www.yahoo.com/entertainment/kristen-bell-on-the-paparazzi-stalking-children-005049108.html.

"Mission Statement," Paparazzi Reform Initiative, 2016. http://www.paparazzi-reform.org/about/mission-statement/.

Modern Museet, Stockholm, Sweden, 1968.

"More Stars Join 'No Kids Policy' Paparazzi Fight," *ETonline*, February 26, 2014, https://www.etonline.com/news/143823_More_Stars_Join_No_Kids_Policy_Paparazzi_Fight.

National Press Photographer's Association, Code of Ethics, accessed on February 27, 2018, https://nppa.org/code-ethics.

New York Civil Rights Law § 79-h (2016).

New York Times v. Sullivan, 376 U.S. 254 (1964).

NY CLS Civ R § 51 (2016).

O.C.G.A. § 24-5-508 (2016).

O'Grady v. Superior Court, 139 Cal. Ct. App 4th. (2006).

Osterreicher, Mickey. (Attorney) in discussion with author, January 2018.

Pittsburgh Press Co. v. Human Relations Commission, 413 U.S. 376 (1973).

Prosser, William L. "Privacy." *California Law Review* 48. (1960).

Puente, Maria. "Celebs push back against the paparazzi," *USA Today*, March 28, 2014, http://www.usatoday.com/story/life/people/2014/03/22/celebs-push-back-against-the-paparazzi/6186163/.

Radio Television Digital News Association Code of Ethics, accessed on February 27, 2018, https://www.rtdna.org/content/rtdna_code_of_ethics.

Raef v. Appellate Division of the Superior County of Los Angeles, 240 Cal. App. 4th 1121 (2015).

Rehm, Emily. "Breaking News and Breaking the Law: Reining in California's Criminalization of Paparazzi and the Intent to Photograph," *Southwestern Law Review*, no. 46 (2017).

Rein, Irving, Kotler, Philip, Hamlin, Michael, and Stoller, Martin. *High Visibility: Transforming Your Personal and Professional Brand* (New York: McGraw Hill, 2006).

Reuters, "California bill protecting children of celebrities from paparazzi signed into law," *Daily News*, September 25, 2013, http://www.nydailynews.com/news/national/halle-berry-jennifer-garner-supported-california-bill-protecting-children-paparazzi-signed-law-article-1.1467192.

Reno v. American Civil Liberties Union, 521 U.S. 844 (1997).

Roca, Teresa. "Watch What Forced Kloe Kardashian to Fire at the Paparazzi After Shopping Trip with Kris and Kendall Jenner," *OK!*, May 12, 2015, http://okmagazine.com/videos/khloe-kardashian-fires-paparazzi-shopping-trip-kendall-jenner-kris-jenner/.

Roitfeld, Carine. "Icons: In Bed with Kim and Kanye," *Harpers Bazaar*, July 28, 2016, http://www.harpersbazaar.com/fashion/photography/a16784/kanye-west-kim-kardashian-interview/. Author's italicization of quotation.

Sattler, Tara. "Comment, Plagued by the Paparazzi: How California Should Sharpen the Focus on Its Not-So Picture Perfect Paparazzi Laws," *Southwest Law Review*, no. 40 (2010).
Schenck v. Pro Choice Network, 519 U.S. 357 (1997).
Schmidle, Nicholas. "The Digital Dirt: How TMZ Gets the Videos and Photos That Celebrities Want to Hide," *The New Yorker*, February 22, 2013, http://www.newyorker.com/magazine/2016/02/22/inside-harvey-levins-tmz.
Smith v. Daily Mail Publishing Co., 443 U.S. 97 (1979).
Society of Professional Journalists, Code of Ethics, accessed on February 27, 2018, http://www.spj.org/ethicscode.asp.
Society of Professional Journalists, "Shield Law 101: Frequently Asked Questions," http://www.spj.org/shieldlaw-faq.asp.
Spears, Britney. "Piece of Me." Jive Records. Originally released November 27, 2007.
Squiers, Carol. "Class Struggle: The Invention of Paparazzi Photography and the Death of Dina, Princess of Wales," *Overexposed: Essays on Contemporary Photography*, ed. Carol Squiers (New York: The New Press, 1999).
Squiers, Carol. "Original Sin: The Birth of the Paparazzo," in *Exposed: Voyeurism, Surveillance, and the Camera since 1870*, ed. Sandra Phillips (San Francisco, CA: San Francisco Museum of Modern Art, 2010).
Stone, Jasmine. "Everyone Loves It When Alec Baldwin Has a Paparazzi Meltdown," *2 Oceans Vibe News*, May 6, 2016, https://www.2oceansvibe.com/2016/05/06/everyone-loves-it-when-alec-baldwin-has-a-paparazzi-meltdown-video/.
Szubiak, Ali. "Kylie Jenner Celebrates 19th Birthday a Full 10 Days Early," *Pop Crush*, August 1, 2016, http://popcrush.com/kylie-jenner-19-birthday-party/.
Tietjin, Alexa. "Jennifer Lopez Blasts Paparazzi After Photo Goes Viral," *WWD*, March 2, 2017, https://wwd.com/eye/parties/jennifer-lopez-blasts-paparazzi-photo-viral-10828622/.
"The Paparazzi Industry," *The Paparazzi Reform Initiative*, http://www.paparazzi-reform.org/industry/.
Trager, Robert, Ross, Susan Dente, and Reynolds, Amy. *The Law of Journalism and Mass Communication* (Los Angeles: Sage, 2016).
Turner, Graeme. "Is celebrity news, news?" *Journalism*, Vol. 15, no. 2 (2014).
U.S. Const. amend. VI.
U.S. v. Eichman, 496 US 310 (1990).
U.S. v. Johnson, 491 US 397 (1989).
U.S. v. O'Brien, 391 U.S. 367 (1968).
U.S. v. Progressive, Inc., 467 F. Supp 990 (1979).
Warren, Samuel D., and Brandeis, Louis. "The Right to Privacy." *Harvard Law Review* (1890).
Wong, Kathleen. "Demi Lovato Returns to Social Media and Calls Out People's Celebrity Obsessions," *Music.Mic*, June 24, 2016, https://mic.com/articles/147035/demi-lovato-returns-to-social-media-and-calls-out-people-s-celebrity-obsessions#.JJu4RuNnU.

Index

About the Author

Joshua N. Azriel is professor of journalism and emerging media at Kennesaw State University. He is the School of Communication and Media's Associate Director of Graduate Studies and directs the M.A. in Integrated Global Communication. He earned his PhD in journalism and communication at the University of Florida. Dr. Azriel teaches journalism and global media courses. His academic research focuses primarily on First Amendment Freedom of Speech and Press issues in the age of digital and social media. He has published numerous academic and legal articles on California's anti-paparazzi laws.

www.ingramcontent.com/pod-product-compliance
Ingram Content Group UK Ltd.
Pitfield, Milton Keynes, MK11 3LW, UK
UKHW020842290926
15470UKWH00004B/1504

9 781498 578974